The Milford Series
Popular Writers of Today
Volume Sixteen
ISSN 0163-2469

DAVID LODGE
How Far Can You Go?

by
Merritt Moseley
University of North Carolina at Asheville

Edited by Dale Salwak

BORGO PRESS / WILDSIDE PRESS

www.wildsidepress.com

THE BORGO PRESS
Publishers Since 1975

*   *   *   *   *   *   *

Library of Congress Cataloging-in-Publication Data

Moseley, Merritt, 1949-
  David Lodge : how far can you go? / by Merritt Moseley ; edited by
Dale Salwak.
    p. cm. — (The Milford series, popular writers of today, ISSN 0163-
2469 ; vol. 16)
  Bibliography: p.
  Includes index.
  ISBN 0-8095-5204-3 : $22.95. — ISBN 0-8095-5229-9 (pbk.)   ;
  1. Lodge, David, 1935- —Criticism and interpretation. I. Title. II.
Series.
PR6062.O36Z77 1991   89-29632
823'.914—dc20   CIP

FIRST EDITION

CONTENTS

PREFACE AND ACKNOWLEDGMENTS

I am happy to be able to write about David Lodge, who has long been one of the most interesting writers in England. He is also one of the more under-appreciated, and I hope that this book will work towards a juster evaluation of his stature as an artist.

My intention has been to write an introduction which would help the reader who knows little about Lodge, without being too elementary for a discourse with the more knowledgable reader. I have thus included some basic information about each of the books along with a modest amount of analysis and evaluation. David Lodge is not only a novelist but a literary critic, whose criticism is eclectic, humane, and lucid. I would be proud to achieve similar qualities in this work.

Although Lodge has not attracted a great deal of critical attention, nevertheless there are some more specialized studies of his novels, which may be found in the Secondary Bibliography. Likewise in various interviews, standard reference books, and (perhaps most helpful of all) essays and introductions by Lodge himself, a reader may flesh out his biography, of which I have given a short account.

I am grateful to Dale Salwak for commissioning this book and thus providing me with the opportunity to make David Lodge's work better known, as well as the enjoyment I have had in working on it.

I owe a debt of gratitude, too, to David Lodge, for his generous cooperation, including permission to quote from copyright materials. My colleagues at the University of North Carolina at Asheville have given me valuable support, particularly Jeff Rackham's encouragement and Michael Gillum's willingness to spend time in fruitful discussions when we both should have been marking essays. At Chester College I have benefitted from the advice and stimulating conversation of Peter Daw. On both campuses I have enjoyed the assistance of the library staff, for which I am thankful. Michele Sands, who wrote on Lodge under my supervision, helped me to clarify my own ideas. Financial assistance from the Undergraduate Research Office and the Mills Fund for Faculty Development in the Humanities has been invaluable.

Finally I thank my family: my daughters — Eleanor, Mary, Claire, and Elizabeth — for bringing delight into my life; and my wife Madeline, whose faith in me and support in a thousand ways make me strong and to whom, in gratitude, this book is dedicated.

Acknowledgments for permission to reprint copyright material

From *The Picturegoers* by David Lodge. Copyright (©) 1960 by David Lodge. Reprinted by permission of Grafton Books, a division of the Collins Publishing Group.

From *Ginger, You're Barmy* by David Lodge. Copyright (©) 1962 by David Lodge. Reprinted by permission of Doubleday, a division of Bantam, Doubleday, Dell Publishing Group, Inc.

From *The British Museum is Falling Down* by David Lodge. Copyright (©) David Lodge, 1965, 1981. Reprinted by permission of Curtis Brown Ltd. and Penguin Books USA Inc.

From *Out of the Shelter* by David Lodge. Copyright (©) 1970, 1985 by David Lodge. Reprinted by permission of Curtis Brown Ltd. and Penguin Books USA Inc.

From *Changing Places* by David Lodge. Copyright (©) 1975 by David Lodge. Reprinted by permission of Viking Penguin, a division of Penguin Books USA Inc.

From *Souls and Bodies* by David Lodge. Copyright (©) 1980 by David Lodge. Reprinted by permission of Curtis Brown Ltd. and Penguin Books USA Inc.

From *Small World* by David Lodge. Copyright (©) 1984 by David Lodge. Reprinted with permission of Macmillan Publishing Company.

From *Nice Work* by David Lodge. Copyright (©) 1987 by David Lodge. Copyright (©) 1988 by David Lodge. Reprinted by permission of Viking Penguin, a division of Penguin Books USA Inc.

CHRONOLOGY

1935	January 28, David John Lodge born in Dulwich, south London
1939	World War II began; Lodge evacuated from London for periods during which he lived in Cornwall & Surrey
1945	returned to London; attended St. Joseph's Academy, Catholic grammar school
1952	graduated from St. Joseph's; entered University College, London, where he read English.
1955	B.A. (Honours) in English. August, drafted into Royal Armoured Corps. Assigned to Catterick Camp in Yorkshire for basic training, then to the R.A.C.'s Driving and Maintenance School at Bovington Camp, Dorset.
1957	discharged from army, began postgraduate study at University College London
1958	*About Catholic Authors*
1959	May 16, married Mary Frances Jacob Received M.A. in English Language and Literature
1959-60	worked as an assistant for the British Council in London, teaching English to foreign students
1960	appointed Lecturer, University of Birmingham *The Picturegoers*
1962	*Ginger, You're Barmy*
1963	"Between These Four Walls," a review written with Malcolm Bradbury and James Duckett, produced in Birmingham
1964-65	lived and traveled in United States on Harkness Commonwealth Fellowship
1965	"Slap in the Middle," a review written with James Duckett and David Turner, produced in Birmingham *The British Museum is Falling Down*
1966	*The Language of Fiction* *Graham Greene*
1967	received Ph.D., University of Birmingham
1969	Visiting Associate Professor, University of California, Berkeley
1970	*Out of the Shelter*
1971	appointed Senior Lecturer, University of Birmingham *The Novelist at the Crossroads* *Evelyn Waugh*

1972	*Twentieth Century Literary Criticism: A Reader*
1973	appointed Reader in English Literature at Birmingham
1975	*Changing Places*
1976	appointed Professor of Modern English Literature, University of Birmingham
1977	*The Modes of Modern Writing*
1980	*How Far Can You Go?*
1981	*Working with Structuralism*
1984	*Small World: An Academic Romance*
1986	*Write On: Occasional Essays '65-'85*
1987	Retired from University of Birmingham
1988	*Nice Work*
	Modern Criticism and Theory: A Reader

Chapter One

INTRODUCTION

David Lodge is the author of eight novels. In addition he has written revues, short fiction, and a considerable body of important academic criticism. The criticism, in particular, is of interest in arriving at a just estimate of his accomplishment, and I will devote some attention to it in its place; but this book is primarily about David Lodge the novelist. Lodge began writing fiction in the 1950's, a time of real excitement and renewal in English literature, a period which may be characterized (a bit simplistically) by reference to "the Movement" in lyric poetry and the school of the "Angry Young Man" in fiction and drama. The Movement was a reaction against the kind of poetry associated with Dylan Thomas: obscure, symbolic, precious, pretentious — as it seemed to the poets of the fifties — and a return to a more down-to-earth, colloquial way of writing which they attributed to Auden and the writers of the Thirties.

The other group of writers, the "Angries," are better known in the United States. The leading names here are John Osborne, whose play *Look Back in Anger* (1956) sounded the klaxon for the "angry" writers, Kingsley Amis (*Lucky Jim*, 1954), John Wain (*Hurry on Down*, 1953), John Braine (*Room at the Top*, 1957), and Alan Sillitoe *(Saturday Night and Sunday Morning*, 1958). Most but not all these writers shared a lower-middle-class background, a secondary and higher education in state-supported schools rather than in the exclusive public schools of an earlier generation of English writers, and an anti-establishment bent that was in some cases explicitly left-wing, in others simply the attitude of the suspicious outsider. Several of the writers later taught at redbrick universities themselves.

David Lodge is about half a generation younger than these, the best known English writers of the fifties. Amis and Philip Larkin had their university years interrupted, or altered, by World War II; the disruption in Lodge's case was of his primary schooling. Lodge published his first novel in 1960. Still there is a strong connection between David Lodge and the writers of the fifties. He has testified to the specific stimulus of their work and the general encouragement he felt from the literary situation at the time. His most powerful tribute is to Amis:

Lucky Jim was another magic book for me — and for most English readers of my age and background, upwardly mobile, scholarship

1

winning, first generation university graduates—for it established precisely the linguistic register we needed to articulate our sense of social identity, a precarious balance of independence and self doubt, irony and hope. (WO 64)

This account sounds like nothing so much as the testimonials, from a generation of English playwrights, to the liberating effect of *Look Back in Anger*.

Beyond the helpful stimulus of *Lucky Jim* Lodge pays tribute to the literary *Zeitgeist* of the middle and late fifties as having helped him to realize himself as a writer.

My own career as a writer — if I may be personal for a moment — was launched very much on the back of the wave started by the Movement, though I was only dimly conscious of this at the time. First of all, the Movement, and the "snowball effect" it had on the literary scene at large, created a mood receptive and encouraging to young aspiring writers: there was a sense of excitement and expectation about literature and drama in England in those days which has not been generated since — and which is not, I think, simply the illusion of middle age looking back at its youth. And to get into this new literary scene one did not need the advantages of a privileged, cultured background, or to have exotic, unconventional or heroic experience to write about. A lower-middle-class South London suburban upbringing, such as I had, was suddenly an almost fashionable background for a young novelist — though not quite as fashionable as a working-class upbringing in a Northern industrial town. (WO 105)

In fact his first novel, *The Picturegoers*, showed very well what could be made of an unexotic, unheroic experience, and it is set squarely in a lower-middle-class South London suburban environment. His second, *Ginger, You're Barmy*, is even closer to the "angry" fiction of the fifties — it is really angry, for one thing, described by its author as an act of revenge — and it examines a part of English experience, National Service, which in its quotidian pointlessness rivals the frustrating details of life in Jimmy Porter's flat or Jim Dixon's Department of History.

I begin by establishing Lodge's kinship with the best-known writers of the fifties, not to pigeonhole him by reference to some "school" but to make two points about his writings. One is that he is, fictionally speaking, a child

2

of the fifties; he shares the realistic and anti-modernist traits of these writers. Writing in 1981 about *Ginger, You're Barmy*, he identified the features it shared with the "angry" fiction:

> gritty realism, exact observation of class and regional differences in British society, a lower-middle or working-class perspective, anti-establishment attitudes, hostility to all forms of cant and pretentiousness, a fondness for first-person, confessional narrative technique. (GYB 216)

The other, more important, point is the versatility, the constant growth, which David Lodge has demonstrated in his career as a novelist. For the fact is that many of the writers who made the fifties an exciting time in English fiction were unable to sustain their achievement. It is true that John Wain and John Braine and Alan Sillitoe have gone on writing novels, but each of them is best known for his first book. Kingsley Amis has had a distinguished career, but is still often thought of as the author of *Lucky Jim*. In part this is bad luck. The Angry Young Man label is, as Amis has insisted, journalist's shorthand, and once a writer is formulated in a phrase like that, he will find it hard not to disappoint. Either he continues to write the same kind of books, but probably not as good as the original (as J. P. Donleavy keeps writing *The Ginger Man*, only worse) or he will write *different* books which confuse and dismay readers *because* they are different. Something like this has happened to Alan Sillitoe. Coming along a little later David Lodge has never been imprisoned by expectations.

But he must be credited, too, with extraordinary willingness to change. There has been an alternation, in his mature novels, between comic fiction and works with a more serious tone: between novels which are playful, self-consciously fictive, and those which hew to the demands of "gritty realism." And, unlike some of the writers of his formative years, David Lodge has continued to get better. Perhaps he has enjoyed the benefits which come to a writer whose first book is not so good that it overshadows the later career. His own judgment of *The Picturegoers*, though it is unnecessarily harsh, reinforces this view.

Any summary of David Lodge's work must acknowledge the broad use of autobiography. Here he explains how a novel begins:

> As far as I am concerned, it begins with an intuition that some segment of my own experience has a kind of thematic unity, and a more than private significance, which might be explored through a

3

fictional story. The novel, in other words, begins as a short answer to the questions that will eventually be asked of it, as of every novel: what is it *about*? (GYB 212)

Lodge has written about almost everything he has ever done. He did two years of National Service, 1955-57, and *Ginger, You're Barmy* is about a two-year National Service stint; he went to Germany, when he was sixteen, to visit his aunt who worked with the American occupation forces, and *Out of the Shelter* is about such a visit by such a youth, though to his sister; he did postgraduate work at University College London, and *The British Museum is Falling Down* is about a man doing just that; and so on. Though the books are *about* segments of David Lodge's experience, the important events of the plots are, as far as one can tell, invented.

There are two facets of Lodge's life which are of such importance in his fiction that they require separate emphasis. One of these is that he is a Roman Catholic; the other is that he has spent his adult life, post-National Service, as an academic. Following the aforementioned two years of postgraduate study, he taught for the British Council for one year, then was employed by the University of Birmingham, at gradually higher ranks in the Department of English, until his retirement in 1987. Though it would oversimplify matters to call Catholicism and the university the two poles of Lodge's mature fiction, nonetheless we cannot talk about him without returning to them again and again.

Catholicism

David Lodge has had much to say about Catholicism, his own and that of others. His first publication was *About Catholic Authors*. He has written monographs on Graham Greene and Evelyn Waugh, both prominent Roman Catholic writers (and both, unlike Lodge, converts). He has been called on to write essays like "Memories of a Catholic Childhood" and "The Catholic Church and Cultural Life," which were published in the Catholic periodical *Tablet* and a book called *The Church Now*. And in almost all of his novels Catholicism has been important. It is most striking in *How Far Can You Go?* which is directly and explicitly about the lives of middle-class Roman Catholics of about David Lodge's age living in Britain. But, until *Nice Work* appeared in 1988, each of his novels has contained Catholic characters, and their conflicts fuel the plots: either conflicts with non-Catholics or conflicts between their spiritual and their secular needs, between the spirit and (the title of Lodge's unpublished juvenile novel) "The Devil, the World, and the Flesh."

4

And yet the Catholic novel as David Lodge writes it is different from what one would expect from Graham Greene or Muriel Spark or Flannery O'Connor. Lodge's books are less mysterious and less theological. Put another way, the concern with Catholic doctrine in them is more practical; the plots derive tension from practical difficulties caused by Catholicism, difficulties which are mostly though not exclusively sexual. Lodge, writing about Evelyn Waugh, defines the Catholic novel:

> This fictional tradition, which goes back to the French Decadence, is characteristically concerned with the operation of God's grace in the world, with a conflict between secular and divine values in which the latter are usually allowed an ironic and unexpected triumph. (EW 30)

Considering Lodge's own books it is easier to see the conflicts between secular and divine values than to detect the operations of God's grace in the world. The divine values involved are, as I have said, usually sexual; the resolution of *Ginger, You're Barmy*, for instance, turns on the use or avoidance of contraception, though the protagonist's failure to use the condoms he possesses is not motivated by religion. That same book contains the ambiguous death of a Roman Catholic Army trainee, and suicide is considered a possibility; but the most interested character, also Catholic, treats this as largely a matter of preserving the comfort of the dead man's family. Roman Catholic doctrine on contraception is crucial in *The British Museum is Falling Down* and *How Far Can You Go?*, present but not crucial in *Changing Places* and *Small World*. *Out of the Shelter* and *The Picturegoers* are partly about the sinfulness of premarital sex, sinfulness felt with particular urgency by the Roman Catholic characters.

And the intervention of divine Grace, if that is what it is, usually takes the mundane form of comic embarrassment. In *The British Museum is Falling Down*, Adam Appleby's intended adultery with a nymphet is not wholly a fleshly value, involved as it is with the prospect of academic advancement. Nevertheless his schemes are overthrown when, trying to buy contraceptives at a chemist's, he runs into Father Finbar, his parish priest; later, no longer interested, he is finding it impossible to fight off the young girl, until she disconcertingly finds that (for complicated domestic reasons), he is wearing women's knickers. In *Small World* the virginal hero Persse decides, in violation of his heartfelt Catholic ethics, to make love to the mysterious Angelica. In acute distress he tries to purchase a packet of Durex condoms; the female clerk provides him with a large box of

5

Farex—disposable diapers. Following this mishap and a disgusting few moments in a pornographic film he flees to a Catholic church and confesses to a priest named, oddly, Father Finbar.

So Lodge uses Catholicism in his fiction as more to do with the facts of Catholic life and less with the mysteries of Catholic faith than most Catholic novelists. He comments on Catholic authors Graham Greene, Muriel Spark, and Anthony Burgess:

> None of these three writers (who would come high on anyone's list of distinguished living English novelists) seems to have any great enthusiasm for, or interest in, the practial effects of Vatican II on Catholic liturgy, devotional practice and general life-styles, both clerical and lay. Indeed, my own novel *How Far Can You Go?* (1980) is, to my knowledge, the first novel to deal directly with that phenomenon in an English context. (WO 36)

This is exactly the kind of contribution to the understanding of Catholicism David Lodge makes; he shows how being Catholic affects one's daily (and, I suppose, nightly) life.

The Academy

David Lodge spent the years 1952-1955 reading English at University College, London; returned there for his M.A from 1957 to 1959; began teaching English in that year, first in London for the British Council and then at the University of Birmingham; and has done so ever since. Thus, aside from National Service and until his retirement in 1987, he has been a university teacher and academic critic. And, as we would expect, given his economical use of his life's experiences in creating the situations — if not the events — of his novels, the academy looms large. The novels can be described as academic in two ways: in one of these, several books embody an academic, literary-critical, meta-fictional approach to fiction, carrying over into the narrative the concerns with narrative that fill the other part of the author's professional life. This "academic" quality, which appears in *The British Museum is Falling Down* and increases in visibility and complexity in the later novels, is part of the discourse of Lodge's fiction. It will be discussed later.

The other "academic" quality of Lodge's fiction is part of the story. Every one of his novels is, at some level of importance, about academic life. The least so is *Out of the Shelter*, which is about a sixteen-year-old boy and his growing maturity; but even this protagonist, Timothy, is revealed

6

in the epilogue to be an environmental scientist with a Ph.D. who is travelling in the United States on a fellowship (as Lodge and his family did in 1964). The primary focal character of *The Picturegoers*, Mark Underwood, is an undergraduate reading English at University College London and a budding aesthete. Nobody in *Ginger, You're Barmy* is an academic; but the narrator Jonathan is doing National Service between undergraduate and postgraduate study, as David Lodge did, though unlike Lodge he foregoes further education and the scholarly career he has planned in favor of a penitential teaching job in an obscure corner of the country. *How Far Can You Go?* is about a large number of men and women, whose lives are traced for twenty-five years. They meet as students, again at London; several of them take up academic posts.

In Lodge's other novels, though, the academic life is much *more* important. *The British Museum is Falling Down* is about a London graduate student, worried about his thesis and about getting a job; *Changing Places* is about an academic exchange between an English don at Rummidge (similar to Birmingham) and an American at Euphoric State (i.e., Berkeley). The same two appear among a crowd of characters in *Small World*, which is about the global business of academic criticism and conference-attending. Here again we see Lodge's use of his own experience. Not only do these three novels demonstrate a rise through the academic ranks, from Adam Appleby, hapless grad student, to Philip Swallow, insignificant member of obscure provincial university, to Philip Swallow, published author, Department Head, and modest globe-trotter. They also use such facts as Lodge's residence at Berkeley in 1969 and his equivocal involvement in the fight over the People's Park, his increasing fame and thus more frequent travel to conferences like the Modern Language Association and the Tel Aviv Conference on the Poetics of Fiction. *Nice Work* divides its focus between two worlds, one of which is the academy; one of its two main characters is a university lecturer, and a literary theorist, whose interests are in key respects the same as David Lodge's; and Morris Zapp and Philip Swallow (now Dean of Arts) reappear, though they are now relatively minor characters.

The question naturally arises, what is the author's attitude toward the academic world in which his novels so often unfold? It is amused but unmalicious. Lodge is aware of the shortcomings of the university and draws them clearly in his books, but he avoids either of the two attitudes toward the university which, to judge from some critics' comments, any thinking person must adopt. One of these is that nothing happens in the sterile world of higher education which is worth writing about, a view

7

echoed in the popular distinction between "going to college" and "the real world." It is not immediately clear why the Army, or journalism, or a whaling ship, or (what is usually meant by "the real world," at least in the United States) business is more "real" than the university. And yet those who comment on the academic novel are given to querulous remarks like that of George Watson, a don himself, who writes that "a university, after all, is a place for students who have barely started to live, and professors who have done all (or nearly all) the living they are ever likely to do." (Watson 42) And he characterizes David Lodge and Malcolm Bradbury as "professors of English in real life, if reality it be." (42) Likewise, J.A. Sutherland includes a chapter on Campus Writers in his *Fiction and the Fiction Industry*, in which he expresses some rather fussy reservations about the campus both as a home for writers and as a subject for their books. Misleadingly quoting Lodge's "Don's Diary" (reprinted in *Write On*), he frets, "is it, one asks portentously, the stuff of fiction? Is there not a lack of necessary tension in the academic lifestyle?" (Sutherland 159) There is no *a priori* answer to such a question; as James said, we must grant the author his *donnée* and ask if good academic novels have been written, and the answer of course is yes. And David Lodge has overcome the disadvantages of the subject, if disadvantages they be (which I doubt), to do his best work in the sub-genre of the academic novel.

Moreover his academic novels have been his most popular books to date. One might think that the portion of the population without higher education would be uninterested in the world of academia; and academics themselves (e.g. Watson) often express distaste for the genre. But as Lodge comments, "In theory, everybody disapproves of academic novels, as being too inbred and stereotyped. In practice there seems to be a very big public for them. People like reading them." (Moseley)

The other conventional attitude, undermined by Lodge's books, is that a book about academia must be a savage satire. Many of them are, of course, but it seems to me that this is often overstated. J. P. Kenyon, a historian at the University of Hull, writes that "it is the dons, the unfortunate lecturers and professors, who really come under the hammer in this kind of novel" (82). He asks why the authors "pillory" the university as they do, and why readers like it. Here is one answer:

> I doubt, in fact, if University Novels are regarded by those who read them as especially relevant to "real" universities. Firstly, the profound cynicism and disgust displayed by their authors is dismissed as a quirk of the cloistered academic. No layman regards a

professor as being quite of this world. (83)

John Schnellenberger reads the University Novel as a key to something larger — the university crisis, a crisis of faith or of commitment — but his conclusions about those novels, again featuring Lodge and Bradbury strongly, are similar: "the comedy is generally of a diminishing, negative type . . . the academic fiction of recent years both portrays and in itself represents evidence of a decline in commitment and purposefulness" (46-47).

It will perhaps be taken as a failure of sensitivity that I, an academic, cannot agree with these generalizations. It is true that Malcolm Bradbury presents a picture of university life considerably darker than Lodge's, a picture in which the worst characters are actually evil rather than silly or vain; that Kingsley Amis's Jim Dixon was wholly unfit for teaching; and that some of the faculty in these books feel a resentment and dislike of some of their students which is, alas, not unknown in real life. But these facts do not add up to the posture of "profound cynicism and disgust" toward the university some have perceived.

Moreover, Lodge's books are less biting than, say, Amis's *Jake's Thing* or Bradbury's *The History Man*. He is writing comedy, after all; comedy traditionally exploits the laughable distance between what men and women are and what they claim to be, between what they pretend to believe and the way they behave, between their spiritual natures and their bodily urges. If no character in Lodge's books is presented as the ideal postgraduate student or university teacher, neither are any of them monstrous or evil. They have shortcomings (as we all do) — perhaps the Catholic Lodge would say that this demonstrates their need for God's grace. Their shortcomings are contained within a comic framework.

Finally one would have to suspect Lodge of great hypocrisy or self-deception if he in fact wrote novels of ruthless denunciation about university life. Asked about his satires of university life in various interviews, he has responded that *Small World* contains

an element of pointing out affectation and hypocrisy, which I think of as the satirical edge of comedy. It's not a censorious kind of satire, but I don't think that in good faith I could satirize in a destructive way an institution which I belong to. I think I can stand back from the academic profession enough to see its absurd and ridiculous aspects, but I don't think it's really wicked or mischievous. That's probably why the overall impression of *Small World* is genial:

9

fun-poking rather than denunciation. (Haffenden 161)

Genial. Fun-poking rather than denunciation. These terms seem to me to capture the tone of *Small World* very ably, and they could be equally applied to *The British Museum is Falling Down* and *Changing Places*. (This is a good place to remark that Lodge, whose interviews, essays, and introductions often comment on his own work, is a remarkably honest, clear-eyed, and sensitive critic of David Lodge. I do not share all his judgments, particularly on the relative value of the books, but he is always illuminating on his influences and his authorial choices.) As for his feeling that he could not savage an institution — the university and English Studies — to which he belongs, another way of putting this would be to say that Lodge could not in good faith belong to an institution which he seriously believed was wicked. Unlike, perhaps, some readers for whom a book which makes fun of aspects of academia is an assault on higher education, Lodge recognizes that it is an institution, with flaws and absurdities, like any other.

I don't think the academic world is all-important or all-embracing as perhaps some of my colleagues do . . .. Any institution or profession is likely to claim an exaggerated importance for itself. I see comedy as a way of puncturing that, and I think it's what comedy always has done. It's done it to politicians and journalists and all kinds of other professions as well as academics. (Marecki 301)

* * * * *

Lodge's Techniques
Again and again David Lodge has insisted on the primacy of language in the making and reading of fiction. Fiction, he has asserted, is made of language, not of life; and when we read and talk about novels, we attend first of all to the words of which they are composed. Obviously this is true. The medium of fiction is words.

It is misleading, in another way, insofar as it suggests that in David Lodge's books the most striking element will be style. He is very far from being negligent about style, in the sense of perspicacious and fluent and colorful language; but he is not one of the writers one thinks of as a word-magician, or the possessor of an immediately distinctive style, like (among living writers) John Updike or Joan Didion or Martin Amis or Norman Mailer. I do not mean to denigrate Lodge's use of language; just to suggest that it is not what first strikes a reader of his novels.

This fact is related to his ongoing concern for the typology of modern British writing. From his first book, *Language of Fiction* (1966), particularly in the chapter of that book called "The Modern, the Contemporary, and the Importance of Being Amis," he has seen modern writing as a dialectic between two "schools" or — more accurately — attitudes. Here he calls them the modern and the contemporary; later he defines essentially the same split as being between modernist and anti-modernist. As he asserts, "the analysis of language is in fact the most precise way of indicating the difference between modern and contemporary writing — and of suggesting the loss involved in shifting from the former to the latter." (LF 245) Lodge recognizes the loss; he is an admirer of Joyce and the other great moderns, and sympathizes with their linguistic aims; and yet, he is a "contemporary," or "basically antimodernist," (WWS 16) — as he acknowledges a bit wistfully, I think. It is part of his heritage as a writer fledged in the fifties, an anti-modernist period indeed in English fiction.

Thus, though he is far from being a careless or graceless stylist, we must look elsewhere for the most distinctive quality in Lodge's fiction. That is its form, its construction, its architectonics. From the beginning of his career, he has been an artful constructor of plot lines, particularly multiple ones; he typically handles a large number of characters, often with no one protagonist; the separate plot lines and characters are related to each other by parallelism, ironic contrast, artful juxtaposition, and other shaping and ordering methods. In his own words (commenting on Evelyn Waugh) he "contains the proliferating growth of his story within a fine mesh of cross reference and recurrence." (EW 44-45)

And this exploration of the possibilities of form is related to another important quality of David Lodge's work: its experimentalism. He is a paradoxical mixture, as I have suggested, of the modernist and anti-modernist; a reader whose "magic books" include both *Ulysses*, the supreme example of experimentation and linguistic daring, and *Lucky Jim*, perhaps the supreme example of traditionalism and assertive anti-modernism. The modern and the contemporary.

In accordance with this pluralistic allegiance, Lodge is what I call an experimental traditionalist. That is, though he has created no new forms *ab novo* like Joyce's (who has?) his restless desire to work with different methods has produced a wide range of formal results. His first novel, *The Picturegoers*, uses a method of coordinating, ordering, and foiling a lot of characters which is similar to the "Wandering Rocks" episode of *Ulysses* or to the linking devices (e.g., the airplane) in *Mrs. Dalloway*. His second,

Ginger, You're Barmy, is structurally indebted to Greene's *The Quiet American*. *Nice Work* is a twentieth-century Condition of England novel, and its form avows its kinship with its great nineteenth-century models. *The British Museum Is Falling Down* is the best example of the combination of tradition and experiment. It contains stylistic pastiches of ten modern authors; its focus on one day and on a man's worry about his wife, who remains at home, is Joycean; and it hews particularly close to *Ulysses*, though with a complicated tonal difference, at the end. But, though this seems derivative, I would insist on the originality of deriving material *in this way*. Joyce, of course, is one of the greatest derivative novelists, and Eliot and Pound's poems are full of borrowing and pastiche. Lodge, in this novel particularly, enacts the modernist relationship with literary history, though now the *history* is itself modernist, and the emotional quality of the relationship is — like so many things in Lodge — ambiguous and complex.

Much of what I have been saying about Lodge's practice may be explained, at least in part, by saying that he is a liberal pluralist. His critical works are strikingly receptive to what is best in various traditions, literary and theoretical, even when this may involve the acceptance of contradiction. Lodge seems to lack completely the urge, so common in today's literary theory (or in that of F. R. Leavis, the leading English figure in twentieth-century English studies) to *rule out*, to strike off, to legislate against. He is inclusive rather than exclusive in his tastes and theories. He is interested in dialectic; but refuses to resolve the dialectic. Recognizing a strong contrast between, say, modernism and anti-modernism, he refuses to endorse one at the expense of the other. Likewise, in the novels, he often works in terms of binary oppositions, but in a way which must frustrate those longing for doctrinaire solutions, he refuses to endorse one term of the opposition, show the "right" belief or character or ideology triumphing over the "wrong" one, or otherwise satisfy our desire to see multiplicity reduced to simplicity.

It is this which has sometimes been called Lodge's "liberalism," and one finds a reaction against it. Reviewing *The Novelist at the Crossroads* (a book, incidentally, in which Lodge asserts that "if the case for realism has any ideological content it is that of liberalism" [33]), Patrick Parrinder comments with unmistakeable condescension:

> As a conscientious liberal critic he recommends the novelist at the crossroads to glance hesitantly to the right and to the left and then to keep straight on, in the faith that on or about December 1960 human character did not change. (879)

12

I have been insisting on the continuity between Lodge's novels (which incidentally began to appear in 1960) and the fiction of the 1950's, a continuity built on a continuing faith in the kind of character which is assumed in those books and even in those of the 19th century. But he is *also* a sympathetic ally (in other books) of John Fowles and Borges and Barth and the metafictionists whose novels rely on no particular idea of human character at all.

This is either frustrating or enriching. To me it is enriching. The openness to complexity, even to contradiction, the refusal to "valorize" one position if that means to demonize the opposing one is, in a perhaps regrettable way, somewhat old-fashioned. While we are surrounded by fashionable madmen who tell us that there is no such thing as truth, such a discovery does nothing to reduce their own dogmatism. Lodge is different. He acknowledges that "I certainly don't think of myself as a dogmatic writer, someone who has a message; I would regard myself as a liberal"; and further specifies what that means:

> I think I am by temperament tentative, sceptical, ironic, and so that reflects itself in the structure and texture of what I write. I am well aware that I tend to play off different ideological or moral attitudes against each other, and I can see that one could say it is evasive . . . . I do sheer away from strong resolutions of the narrative line in my novels which would affirm one position rather than another. I tend to balance things against each other; my novels tend towards binary structures — with, for example, opposite characters — and they very much leave the reader to make up his own mind. (Haffenden 152)

There are many people who would define the adjective "liberal" as only another word for "well-meaning but indecisive," and Marxist critic Terry Eagleton has defined liberalism as "the impotent conscience of a bourgeois society" (Haffenden 51); for them such remarks as Lodge's will be confirmation. Lodge means something more honorable, more in the Matthew Arnold vein of liberalism — the refusal to believe in the "one thing needful," a determination to see all sides of issues — that is admirably catholic in understanding and sympathy. It is an essential quality in his criticism and in his novels, particularly those which are most binary in construction, as well.

13

Chapter Two

BIOGRAPHY

David John Lodge was born on January 28, 1935, in Dulwich, South London.[1] He was the only son of William Frederick and Rosalie Murphy Lodge; his mother was a Roman Catholic and his father was a "non-Catholic," so that he was considered the offspring of a mixed marriage. Mr. Lodge played in dance bands in the West End of London. The family lived in a neighborhood near the borders of New Cross and Brockley which Lodge has described as a drab late-nineteenth century suburb of London, declining streets of large Victorian houses broken up into flats, with a "little street of rather small semi-detached houses built in the 1930s" where the Lodges lived (Moseley). His parents chose the location because the all-night trams ran that far out from central London, permitting his father to travel home from his engagements as a musician.

The Lodge home was near the docks of the East End, and the bombing was heavy after war broke out in 1939. William Lodge was in the RAF, and David and his mother were periodically evacuated from their home, spending some time in Cornwall and Surrey. His primary education was also somewhat disrupted by the war and by his family's dislocation, and he received part of his schooling as one of two boys in a convent school under relaxed wartime regulations. All his education was in Catholic schools. When the war ended he attended St. Joseph's Academy, a Catholic grammar school in Blackheath.

At sixteen Lodge went to Germany to visit his aunt, who was working for the American army of occupation. This was an important opportunity for the boy to see a side of life other than the rather cramped view dictated by his background and the privations of postwar England, and an altered version of it is the main action of *Out of the Shelter* (1970). At seventeen he entered University College, London, to read English. He says that he "floundered" there (Haffenden 149), but he earned a first-class degree in 1955. He also met Mary Frances Jacob, his future wife.

He was offered a grant to pursue post graduate study; he accepted it but deferred it until after his national service, then required of all able-bodied young men. National Service for Lodge meant two years in the Royal Armoured Corps, spent first at Catterick Camp in Yorkshire for basic training and then at the RAC's Driving and Maintenance School at Bovington Camp in Dorset. He hated his national service, particularly that part of it spent at Catterick, which features in *Ginger, You're Barmy*.

14

Released from the army in 1957, he returned to University College London where he spent two years and produced an MA thesis on the Catholic novel. There being no word limit at that time, he explains, he wrote a 700-page thesis. There is now a limit, for which, he implies, he is partly responsible. He received his MA in 1959.

In May of that year he married Mary Jacob. Failing to find a teaching position in a University, he worked for the British Council in London, teaching English to foreigners.

In 1960 several important things happened. His first child, Julia, was born. (She was followed by Stephen in 1962 and Christopher in 1966.) He was appointed, rather fortuitously, to a one-year replacement lecturership in the English Department at the University of Birmingham. The following year his appointment was converted to permanent status, and he continued at Birmingham until his retirement in 1987. In 1971 he was made Senior Lecturer, in 1973 Reader, and in 1976 Professor of Modern English Literature.

Also in 1960 his first novel, *The Picturegoers*, was published. It was well enough received to encourage him to go on with novel-writing. Based on his own life during his studies at University College London, it is out of favor with the author, who considers it sentimental, and has been out of print for a number of years. (It is, at this writing, the only one of David Lodge's seventeen books which *is* out of print).

From this time forward David Lodge has maintained a dual career as, on the one hand, a University don and academic critic, and on the other an author of novels. His first critical book, *Language of Fiction*, appeared in 1966, and in 1967 he was awarded a Ph.D. by the University of Birmingham on the basis of that book. The other novels and academic books which have appeared steadily may be found in the Primary Bibliography.

In 1963 he collaborated with James Duckett and Malcolm Bradbury on a comic revue, *Between These Four Walls*, which was produced in Birmingham. Bradbury, also an academic specializing in the modern novel and a novelist, was then Lodge's colleague at Birmingham; they are close friends, their careers have been "curiously interlinked" (Moseley), and Bradbury's removal, soon afterwards, to the University of East Anglia was perhaps a good thing for both of them in permitting greater independence. Lodge has credited his participation in the revue with liberating his comic and satiric gifts, which contributed greatly to his next novel, *The British Museum is Falling Down*. He worked on another comic revue, *Slap in the Middle*, which was staged in 1965.

Lodge has spent two extended periods in the United States. The first came when he received a Harkness Commonwealth Fellowship, for travel and residence in the U.S., in 1964-65. He spent the first part of his stay in Providence, Rhode Island, then traveled across the country in a rented car, and spent the last part of the year in San Francisco. This year was clearly an enjoyable and liberating experience, and Lodge's attitude toward the United States, which forms an important part of novels like *Out of the Shelter*, *Changing Places* and *Small World* and appears in some of the personal essays collected in *Write On*, is very sympathetic, unusually so for a contemporary English intellectual. In 1969 he returned, this time as a visiting Associate Professor at the University of California at Berkeley. He arrived at the most interesting possible time to be at Berkeley, or on the West Coast: at the height of the "youth revolution," with its antiwar and anti-university-administration phases. Without, perhaps, putting flowers in his hair, Lodge did become involved in events like the struggle for the People's Park, and this rich experience has also contributed to his American scenes, notably in *Changing Places*.

The twin careers of novelist and academic critic both moved in a steady, even if not smooth or spectacularly sharp, rising curve between 1960 and 1988. With the exception of *Out of the Shelter*, which was something of a flop, his novels were well received in England and sold well. The "breakthrough" was *Changing Places*, which won greater sales in England, "astonishing reviews," and several literary prizes (Moseley). *How Far Can You Go?* sold better, and won the Whitbread Prize (the proceeds of which enabled Lodge to reduce his teaching to half-time in 1981). And *Small World* was something of a best-seller, being, moreover, made into a television series broadcast on the Independent Television Network in 1988. *Nice Work*, published in October, 1988, was (like *Small World*) on the short list of finalists for the Booker Prize, and it is also a best-seller.

Small World was the first of his books to be successful in the United States, where his reception has been much more modest. *The Picturegoers* was never published in America; *Ginger, You're Barmy* was, without much effect; *The British Museum is Falling Down* appeared as a paperback under the title *Vatican Roulette*; *Changing Places* did not achieve an American publication for several years, despite its American topicality; *How Far Can You Go?* also appeared under a different title (*Souls and Bodies*) and was, in Lodge's words, "another debacle." He has had five different American publishers, and in general, as he sums it up, his experiences of publishing in American have been "very odd, and on the whole disappointing" (Moseley).

Recently Lodge has turned his attention to writing drama. Channel

16

Four in England commissioned him to adapt *Out of the Shelter* for television, but decided against filming it; he has written a play called *The Pressure Cooker* which is likely to be produced in the West End soon; and the BBC will broadcast a televised version of his most recent novel *Nice Work*, for which he is writing the script.

He is now, at age fifty-five, fully retired from the University of Birmingham and he will probably write no more books of academic criticism, though he continues to review. He is, thus, for the first time in his life, a full-time writer and, given his fertility of invention, will continue to be, what he now has clearly become, one of the major contemporary English authors.

NOTES

1 The best available sources on David Lodge's biography are Dennis Jackson's article in *British Novelists Since 1960, Part 2: A-Z*, which is Volume 14 of the *Dictionary of Literary Biography*; the article and interview by Joan E. Marecki and Jean W. Ross in *Contemporary Authors, New Revision Series, Volume 19*; and the interview with Lodge in John Haffenden's *Novelists in Interview*. There is a good deal of Lodge's life, of course, in such novels as *Out of the Shelter* and *Ginger, You're Barmy*; the recently added afterwords to those novels help to establish which parts of them are autobiographical. Essays like "Memories of a Catholic Childhood" and "The Bowling Alley and the Sun, *or* How I Learned to Stop Worrying and Love America," reprinted in *Write On: Occasional Essays '65-'85*, are very illuminating. I am also indebted to a long conversation with Mr. Lodge in September 1988.

Chapter Three

BEGINNING
THE PICTUREGOERS

David Lodge's first novel was published in 1960 and, alone among his books, has never been reprinted. Lodge's own comments on it suggest that it has lost favor with its author as well as, presumably, with the reading public. He describes it in the recent essay "My Joyce" as "an immature work, mostly written some years before it was published, which I cannot read now without embarrassment" (WO 61). I am not sure why Mr. Lodge finds reading this novel embarrassing; in fact it is a fine beginning, a serious book on serious themes, and impressive work for a writer who was only twenty-five when it was published and some years younger when he wrote it.

It contains some remnants of "The Devil, The World, and The Flesh," the novel Lodge wrote when he was eighteen, also set in a seedy South-London suburb and focusing on Roman Catholics. There is also reason to believe that in the Mallorys, a large, mostly comfortable Catholic family with whom Mark Underwood lodges, he is incorporating traits of the Jacobs, the large family of Mary Jacob, whom Lodge married in 1959. Lodge says that the Mallorys are "a romanticized, idealized version of my wife's family, really" (Moseley).

Add to these facts that Mark Underwood, who is the closest thing to a protagonist in the large cast of characters, is a student of English at University College London (as Lodge was when he wrote the first version of the book), and it is clear that in this novel, as in all the rest of his books, especially the early ones, he is staying close to his own experiences. The pattern is set. From here on out the David Lodge novel will make use of some significant element of his own life, though more for setting or milieu or background or occasion than for the events of the plot. Academic and Catholic concerns will blend in some proportion. Here Catholicism predominates, as in several of the later books it is academic life. Perhaps more important, we can see already Lodge's great interest in *pattern*. The management of a large number of characters, the use of contrasting themes, the handling of juxtaposition and contrast, the quasi-musical use of counterpoint, the employment of certain settings, chiefly the cinema, as nodes; all this is highly skilled.

The complex interweaving of characters and themes does produce a book that some readers have found difficult to follow clearly (Jackson 471), and it is not easy to summarize. The novel is essentially about the Mallory family, two young men who impinge on their lives, and others who attend either the same cinema or the same church. The most important Mallorys are Tom and Bett, the parents — she a devout Catholic, he a less-devout convert — Patrick and Patricia, teenagers enacting mild rebellions, and Clare, a former novice in a religious order who has returned to a home, and a secular world, in which she is conspicuously naive and ill at ease. Five more Mallory children hardly figure in the plot except to furnish a large warm family. Damien O'Brien, an Irish cousin of the Mallorys, lives next door and loves Clare. Unfortunately he is repulsive. Moreover, he is an ex-seminarian (as Clare is an ex-convent girl) and in him the Catholicism has become twisted and dark and ugly. In his black moods, his forceful but only partly successful suppression of his own instincts, and his resentment of Mark Underwood, he is much like Dickens's Bradley Headstone in *Our Mutual Friend*.

The household is completed by Mark Underwood, who lodges with the Mallorys. He is the novel's major figure, at least if we measure by the proportion of the text taken up with his thoughts and actions and by the appearance of "authority" given to the passages in which he reflects on life. Mark is a lapsed Catholic, from a suburb called Blatcham slightly south and, we can infer, higher on the social scale. As the novel opens Mark is a skeptic and a sarcastic aesthete, full of contempt for the petty-bourgeois people around him, though from time to time he feels a pang of self-disgust as well. He keeps a notebook and wants to be a novelist. His Stephen Dedalus qualities are undercut by the book's demonstration that he is really rather conventional, not the rebel he fancies himself; and, when he writes a poem about Clare, it is no villanelle but a bit of doggerel he titles "On Hearing His Beloved's Urination."

The other characters who figure significantly in the book are Father Kipling, the parish priest; Harry, a knife-wielding, woman-hating spiv; Len and Bridget, sweethearts divided by conditions; and Doreen, an usherette at the Palladium cinema who eventually becomes pregnant by Mr. Berkeley, the manager.

The novel is divided into three sections: two long parts and a shorter coda. Each is a slice taken through the minds of many different people, the external events rendered through the eyes of these characters and, in some measure, in their words. Part One is the first night and the following day. It begins with all the people in the novel converging on the Palladium Theatre, where they are to see an American extravaganza called *While the*

Cat's Away, starring Amber Lush. There is a good deal of ironic counter-point to their thoughts; for instance, those of Mr. and Mrs. Mallory, who are arriving together at the cinema. We learn that Mrs. Mallory is more religious than her husband, also the more crucial fact that she is worried about a lump on her breast which may turn out to be cancer. The most thoroughly transmitted thoughts are those of Mark Underwood, who is accompanying Clare Mallory to the pictures, which give us the necessary exposition of the kind of man he is. There is also an ironic counterpoint here, this time between his thoughts and the disguised version of them he communicates to Clare. That is, our view of his mind reveals the hypocriti-cal game he is playing. He is determined to seduce Clare, and for this purpose he has decided to affect a greater faith than he in fact feels. He is a faltering Catholic, so he knows how to pretend. The constant foiling of his thoughts and his speeches demonstrates clearly the measure of his pretense. By contrast, Clare is almost unnaturally transparent: we learn that she knows nothing of pretense, even of makeup or (as her sister wryly observes) the kind of underwear which would make the most of her potentially splendid figure. (Mark, by the way, has detected the potential in her body despite its lack of proper support and shaping.)

These are the most important characters at the evening's showing of the film, though we are also privy to glimpses into the minds of Len and Bridget, Harry, two younger Mallorys, Mr. Berkeley, some cleaning staff, and a good many others.

This tapestry weaves together some startlingly diverse threads. There are the thoughts of Harry, the violent sociopath who is somewhat reminis-cent of Graham Greene's Pinkie, as he snarls his hatred of "tarts" and rips up the upholstery with his switchblade. We share the sad reflections of Mr. Berkeley about the decline of the Palladium — he remembers when it was a great live theatre, and it has declined to a run-down picture palace. Most amusing is the discomfiture of Father Kipling; having come to the Pal-ladium to see *Song of Bernadette* he stays to watch *When the Cat's Away*, and despite his shocked reaction, his refusal to believe that people actually watch such stuff, it is made clear that he is sexually aroused by the movie. The next day — in expiation, as it seems — he launches a crusade against the pictures, urging his parishioners to attend a Saturday evening service instead. Predictably it fails.

As the evening ends Mark tries to fondle Clare's breast, but is repulsed; Damien O'Brien eavesdrops biliously on them; Harry follows Bridget and scares her.

Saturday Night and Sunday Morning had been published already, or it

20

would have made a good title for this novel, or at least for part one, for it continues with the Sunday morning after the Saturday night at the pictures. This develops the analogy which runs through the book between religion and entertainment, the Church and the picture palace, the decline of Christianity and the decline of show business: Mr. Berkeley and Father Kipling are in some ways competitors — Fr. Kipling would say so, at any rate — but they are kindred souls in presiding over an institution in sad decline, a ceremony no longer so meaningful in a seedy edifice. Mark Underwood reflects during the film:

> It was in a way a substitute for religion — and indeed a fabulously furnished pent-house, and the favours of awesomely shaped women, offered a more satisfactory conception of paradise than the sexless and colourless Christian promise — the questionable rapture of being one among billions of court-flatterers. (58)

Mark's view of what religion offers is a jaundiced one at this stage, but Lodge makes clear that just as the cinema holds out different attractions to different picturegoers — for some a place to be alone and kiss, for others just a soft seat and a place to rest away from the house and the children — so religion has its own diverse appeals.

Part two is another passage of about a hundred pages, showing the state of play with the same characters some months later. Mark and Clare are in an odd sort of evolution; she is secularizing, he is sanctifying. That is, she is moving toward an accomodation with the world and with him; his religion, at first pretended, seems to be becoming more real. Father Kipling has begun his campaign to boycott the pictures, without success (though Bett Mallory attends his new Saturday evening service). Len and Bridget's frustrations have become more severe; at first just separated by lack of access to each other — they live at a distance, he has to catch a bus and can't walk her home, and so on — they now face a greater separation caused by his callup to do his National Service.

In this section Harry attacks Bridget as she walks home alone, but she drives him off by biting his hand. The adolescent rebellion of Patricia Mallory is developed in this part of the novel. Mark lends her a copy of *A Portrait of the Artist as a Young Man*, and she identifies with Stephen Dedalus. By now, Mark's angry-young-aesthete role has faded, and he tries to discourage Patricia's uprising against family and church.

The final short section of the novel resolves many of the strands of plot. The Palladium, surprisingly, is a roaring success, for it is now the rock and

21

roll era; *Rock Around the Clock* is showing, the theatre is packed, and Mr. Berkeley is at last successful. Another of his successes — the seduction of Doreen, one of his employees — has borne unfortunate fruit as she is pregnant and headed north to have the baby. Harry has found his niche — he is a rocker, and as we see him last he is at the films and even has a girlfriend.

The two love stories we have been following are resolved in sharply contrasting ways. Len and Bridget have decided to marry before he goes off to training at Catterick, though they know that perhaps they should wait. Mark and Clare have by now roughly changed positions. Clare has accomodated herself to the world, wears makeup, shows an interest in sexual matters. She is ready for a sensual love affair, but now *he* resists because of religious scruples. In a scene which parallels Part One, Clare now places Mark's hand on her breast and he withdraws it. In fact, he explains, he is going to become a priest, going to join the Dominicans. The state of Mark's faith at this position is not clearly established, and he doesn't seem fully committed to the priestly life. It is entirely possible that he is now entering another phase of shallow commitment to a role; as he began the novel wearing the Latin Quarter clothing of a young artist, he now changes into the Dominican garb — but, I cannot help believing, not for good and not for long.

Meanwhile Mrs. Mallory has discovered some of Mark's early writings about Clare, including the urination poem, upbraids him for them, and he makes this a pretext for departure. We last see him visiting his dismal parents at Blatcham. Clare, undone by developments, wanders (significantly) first to the movies then to the church, where she meets Len and Bridget who are getting married; she witnesses the wedding, loans them money and finds them lodgings.

* * * * *

This is indeed a lot of plot. Many characters move through these pages; others move just along the edge of the story — such a one is a certain Mabel, who is named as a friend of the daughter of one of the maids at the Palladium and as a friend of Harry's girl in Part Three. Whether the girl and the daughter are the same we cannot be certain, though it seems likely.

In addition to the large number of people there are, as my summary shows, several plots unreeling at the same time, plots which for the most part are connected with each other only by juxtaposition and alternation, and by tacit thematic contrasts and comparisons. It is possible to feel, also,

22

that the novel ends unsatisfactorily, that the reversal of Mark and Clare's positions is all very well but that both are left in the air, that Patricia's promising rebellion comes to no clear end, that Mr. and Mrs. Mallory are left hanging (though Bett's lump proves benign). I believe that such dissatisfactions are misplaced. This novel is very much in the social-realist vein (perhaps signalled by the showing of *The Bicycle Thieves* at the Palladium in Part Two) of the fifties; as a slice of life it differs from naturalism in its internal rather than external focus, but it has the same refusal of tidy endings. The tidy endings the novel does have are all in some way problematical; Mark's new path is not necessarily the right course for him. Len and Bridget, though they marry, have purchased problems for themselves and they end on a gloomy note. Harry has become normal; but is this not a critique of normality? And the happy ending for the Palladium — is that what it is? Mr. Berkeley, wistfully longing for the departed days of the live theatre, has enthusiasm and custom again with *Rock Around the Clock*; but will it ever be the same? And, to preserve the parallel between church and cinema, we see a factitious kind of religion at the end as well; Mabel and her mother have been "saved" at a Billy Graham rally.

This is just one sign of the finely sketched detail and texture of this novel. Lodge captures the place and the time. There are a number of understated period touches, and though this is not a novel of social history, a good deal of it is woven in. For just one example, consider the movies which play the Palladium in the three parts. In Part One, though Father Kipling thinks he is going to see *Song of Bernadette*, a 1943 movie featuring Jennifer Jones, the film is *When the Cat's Away*. This title, invented by David Lodge to permit the broad satire of Amber Lush and the mindlessness of the film, also has a late forties sound. In Part Two the film is *The Bicycle Thieves*, the neo-realist classic by Vittorio de Sica, made in 1949: obviously a different sort of picture entirely from the Amber Lush vehicle. In the last section *Rock Around the Clock*, starring Big Bill Haley and the Comets and dating from the middle fifties, is showing. The films have moved us from the war years on to the period when rock and roll is just coming in and (though this novel contains no hint of it) television will soon become the family's entertainment anodyne. Thus, though the time covered by the novel is only about a year, at most, the range of films gives it, through allusion, a broader sweep.

Just as impressive is the novelist's treatment of the setting. This tellingly-named Brickley is no slum; but it is dull and ugly and — this is the point — completely ordinary. Mark Underwood analyzes his first feelings for

the grimy, arid streets of Brickley; for the tall decaying Victorian houses, from each of whose windows sagged the washing of a different family; for the long, maddening rows of squat, identical nineteenth-century workers' homes with big new cars parked outside in incongruous opulence; for the worn, soft pavements; and for the honourable scars of the blitz, of the suffering he knew only by repute, the patches of new bricks, slates, paving-stones, the pre-fabs sprouting like mushrooms from the dung of destruction, new raw blocks of flats, and even the occasional neglected bomb-site, its stark outlines softened by the work of weather and vegetation, a playground for children, and for him a kind of shrine too. (42)

The point encapsulated here, of the ordinariness of life in Brickley, throbs through this book. Lodge has often referred to himself as a child of a lower-middle-class South London suburb, and this milieu, then, is the world of his youth. His dedication to realism helps to explain this choice of setting. But there is something else, and it comes out strongly in the novel's emphasis on the everyday reality of Roman Catholicism. Lodge has noted elsewhere that most English Catholic novelists have come to it as something exotic:

Most of these figures were converts to Catholicism, and many of them were attracted to the Church precisely by its cultural heritage. But that cultural heritage was Continental European — or, if English, medieval. Catholicism, to most of these men, meant Dante, Aquinas, Gothic cathedrals, Renaissance painting, Baroque architecture, orchestral masses, the organic, pre-industrial society. (WO 33)

But David Lodge insists that Catholicism is not like that at all. Having grown up in what he calls the "Catholic ghetto," in which Catholicism is the very antithesis of the exotic, he is well placed to give us passages like this, describing the ecclesiastical life in Brickley:

The common mistake of outsiders, that Catholicism was a beautiful, solemn, dignified, aesthetic religion. But when you got inside you found it was ugly, crude, bourgeois. Typical Catholicism wasn't to be found in St. Peter's or Chartres, but in some mean, low-roofed parish church, where hideous plaster saints simpered along the wall, and the bored congregation, pressed perspiration-tight into the pews, rested their fat arses on the seats, rattled their beads, fumbled for their smallest change, and scolded their children. Yet in their presence God was made and eaten all day long, and for that reason those people could never be quite like other people, and that was Catholicism. (173)

* * * * *

I have commented already on Lodge's tendency toward binary or dialectical structure in his novels. This trait is already apparent in *The Picturegoers*. A few of the oppositions will make the point: Damien O'Brien the ex-seminarian plays the foil for Clare Mallory, the ex-novice; he also contrasts with Mark Underwood, who is religiously insincere but presentable while Damien is devout but appalling. The most important dialectic involving characters is, of course, that which pairs Mark and Clare in a sharply ironic reversal: he goes from wordly to unwordly while she treads the opposite path; his interest in sex wanes as hers waxes; she comes out of a religious order, he makes plans to enter one. (Presumably there was some point where the two curves intersected, where they were of like mind, but they missed it and the novel does not present that moment.)

And the major thematic dialectic, a complicated one because Lodge is as concerned to underline similarities as to point differences, is of course that between church and cinema. He shows this from a number of angles so that eventually we are aware of the comparisons, aware that the picturegoers attend religiously and the churchgoers look for an element of entertainment. These contrasts make themselves, with a little help from the thoughts of Mark Underwood. And they make themselves as a result of the author's method of construction, which is that of reticent interweaving of vignettes. Holding them in suspension together because all the people involved are attending the same movie, he presents us with many separate views into the characters' minds, presented in *style indirect libre*, for the most part. One obvious model for this technique, as Lodge explains that he recognizes "now," is *Ulysses*:

In the way the narrative "cuts" from one character to another as they walk about the streets of the South London suburb where the action is set, often oblivious of each other's existence, but impinging directly or indirectly on each other's lives, and in the way the narrative discourse is focalized through these characters, and their

consciousness rendered in an idiom appropriate to each – in all this
I now perceive the model of the "Wandering Rocks" episode of
Ulysses. (WO 65)

This is exactly right, both in its description of the method and in its
acknowledgment of the source. But note Lodge's use of the word "cuts" to
describe the rapid interchanges between the vignettes. This points toward
cinematic technique (an influence on Joyce, as well). In his novels and his
critical work Lodge has shown a continuing interest in film, and he has
recently written screenplays; what more fitting, given the subject matter,
than a cinematic technique in *The Picturegoers*? Park Honan, in an essay
called "David Lodge and the Cinematic Novel in England," writes about
The Picturegoers, as well as Lodge's next two books, labeling them
"cinematic," but missing, I cannot but feel, the obvious point of crosscutting. He is using the term to mean internal focalization:

In *The Picturegoers* the novelist's own camera – in that familiar
maneuver of impressionism – is set behind the characters' eyes. . .
But the viewpoints are not developed in the showily imitative
fashion of dialogue. Instead there is a subtle shift between kinds of
vocabularies as viewpoints change. (171)

Honan goes on to make a distinction between cinematists and stylists;
the first group, including Lodge, use language in a transparent way; the
language is not foregrounded. This distinguishes them from the stylists –
Joyce is singled out – in whose writing the style calls attention to the artist.
Perhaps this is a valid distinction (and many would argue that some
foregrounding of language is an essential property of *literature*), and
perhaps Lodge is correctly placed on the cinematic (i.e., realistic) side of
the divide. Still this is inflating an old distinction (well covered in Lodge's
chapter on the modern and the contemporary in *Language of Fiction*) and
wasting the notion of the "cinematic" novel.

In a more important way a cinematic novel is one which is constructed
like a film. That is to say, it has a minimum of connective exposition or
summary, and it uses cutting and juxtaposition (the *and-then* function) to
achieve the effects (for instance irony or correction) which traditional
narrative would assign to omniscient commentary or analysis. Lodge will
return to the cinematic technique again, presenting parts of both *How Far
Can You Go?* and *Changing Places* in the form of scripts, where he will
exploit other advantages which film possesses over written narrative.

Chapter Four

SCRUPULOUS REALISM
GINGER, YOU'RE BARMY

Len, one of the second-rank characters in *The Picturegoers*, is doing his national service at Catterick Camp in Yorkshire. He explains why he hates it, instancing the prevalence of rats and sheep dung, but insists that

"It's not the conditions I mind so much though . . . it's the officers and N.C.O.s. The way they treat you. Like bits of dirt. 'Go here, go there, do this, do that. Double!' And their stupid wisecracks. 'Did you shave this morning? Well, put a blade in the razor next time.' Blimey, the times I've heard that! And you can't do a thing. Not a thing." (221)

Not surprisingly David Lodge did his national service at Catterick. And one could argue that in his second novel, *Ginger, You're Barmy* (1962), he proved Len wrong. For that book focuses on a man who rebels against the mindless dehumanization of basic training and does something. And we can also see David Lodge "doing something" – avenging himself for the miseries of his own National Service – by writing the book.

It is the story of two men and two times. The narrator, Jonathan Browne, is a conventional young man, whose life is in some details like that of his creator. That is, he has taken a first class degree in English at University College London, plans to do postgraduate study there, but has interrupted his education to do his National Service. He detests the army, but he gets along with it, adjusting to its brutality and eventually having a fairly easy two years' tour of duty. His opposite number is Mike Brady, a ginger-haired nonconformist; a more complicated, more principled man though his principles are sometimes unclear, a man who cannot fit into the army. Mike is also a believing Catholic, unlike Jonathan who calls himself an agnostic, and an Irishman. The two share, though serially rather than simultaneously, a girl, Pauline.

Jonathan, the narrator, manipulates the two time scales of the novel. In present time Jonathan is living through his last weekend in the military, making plans to take Pauline (his girl now) on holiday to Majorca and to advance their frustrating sexual relationship by deflowering her. The past time focuses on the early months of his and Mike's National Service, and is mostly about Mike. The two narratives are interwoven, as flashbacks float up into Jonathan's mind throughout his last days in the army.

The best scenes are those which describe the onset of basic training at the Catterick camp. Here Lodge very vividly documents the mindless brutality of the life. Mike and Jonathan are educated; this makes them candidates for officers' training (a choice they eventually reject in an act of revolt) but also makes them targets for the abuse and suspicion of the rest of the men, mostly working-class and portrayed as almost animalistic. But these two suffer less from the warfare between the classes, between the somewhat refined and the coarse, than another young man, named Percy Higgins, who is wholly unfit for the army.

Percy is privileged (he comes from an "Old Catholic" country family, perhaps of the type Evelyn Waugh celebrated), dim, physically hopeless. He attracts attention by kneeling to say his prayers and objecting to casual blasphemy. He cannot march or shoot a rifle. Physically and emotionally delicate, he attracts the contempt of his training officer and the rougher elements in his squad.

The central events of the plot of this book are precipitated by Percy. Threatened, because of his incompetence as a recruit, with being forced to repeat basic training, and unbalanced by the constant mistreatment, he shoots himself on the rifle range. He has either committed suicide or (the explanation which comes to seem most likely) was trying to shoot off his trigger finger in order to escape the military. His death, in this case, is no more than another of his foulups. Though it chastens the whole squad for some time, it particularly engages Mike Brady's energies. First, as a Roman Catholic, he understands the spiritual ramifications of suicide, and is concerned that the death be ruled accidental; on the other hand, and illogically, he wants Percy's corporal Baker punished for his mistreatment of Percy (which would be relevant only if Percy *had* committed suicide). Mike reacts to the inquest's failure to blame Baker by writing a letter to the *Times*. Eventually he assaults Baker, is jailed, and escapes with the aid of the IRA. As Mike's life becomes more melodramatic, Jon's settles down; though he remains openly loyal to Mike, he quickly takes over Pauline; and by doing enough to get by he "succeeds" as a short-time soldier. This is the past narrative.

The present is deceptively humdrum; in it Jon finds that he has to stand guard duty his last night in the army; while he is on duty there is a raid on the camp which Jon more or less accidentally foils. It turns out to be a weapons-snatch by the IRA and Mike is among them. Jon speaks to Mike once more, then departs the army for Pauline and Majorca. His last act is to flush away the condoms bought in preparation for their holiday.

This account is a bit misleading, for there is actually a third time here; the account I have given omits the prologue and epilogue, in which it is made clear that, in *prologue-time*, it is three years after Mike's arrest; that the casual disposal of the contraceptives led to Pauline's pregnancy and to marriage; that Pauline's pregnancy also induced in Jonathan "what most people would call a nervous breakdown, and some perhaps a spiritual crisis" (209); that Mike was imprisoned; and that, most dramatic of all, Jon has put off postgraduate study in order to move to a barbaric cottage in the remote corner of England where Mike is in prison. The central narrative, the epilogue explains, was in fact written in Majorca while Pauline lay ill with food poisoning. It was only after the book was finished that Jon "succeeded" in a moment of joyless sex which impregnated Pauline. It should be clear from this overview that this is another plot-rich novel, fertile in inventive ways of arranging the material. Like many novels in which a narrator tells the story of another who is the apparent protagonist (*The Great Gatsby, Heart of Darkness, Bartleby the Scrivener, Moby Dick*), it is really as much about the narrator's perceptions and his moral development as about the things the other character does. The twin narrative lines insist on this fact. We are constantly being asked to filter our knowledge of Mike through the mind of Jon, a mind which is at times self-satisfied, more often uneasy. For here, as in *The Picturegoers*, we have a pattern of two dialectical worlds, the civilian world and the army world. Jon comments on them when he says

> For us soldier-commuters "home" and "camp" were two disparate and self-contained worlds, with their own laws and customs; every week we passed from one to the other and back again, changing like chameleons to melt into the new environment. (121)

And we have a dialectic of two characters in Jon and Mike. Their differences are obscured by their early companionship as the two sensible middle-class characters in their platoon, with a shared university background. But as Jon comes to realize, he is very different from Mike, who is Catholic, imprudent, experienced and impulsive where Jon is fashionably agnostic, a prig with a sharp understanding of where his bread is buttered and what he must do to get ahead. From time to time he plays a beam of self-analysis upon himself. "I have always tried to avoid occasions for regret, the most lingering of all the unpleasant emotions, by prudent foresight," he primly notes as he calculates whether making love to Pauline would be wise or not (43). Later, explaining the philosophy which permitted his successful adaptation to the army, Jon thinks that "all human activity was useless, but some kinds were more pleasant than others" and philosophizes that

> Success consisted in determining which box would be most pleasant for you, and getting into it. If you were forced to inhabit an unpleasant box for a time, then you could make it as comfortable as possible until you could get out. Luck or cunning were the most effective attributes in this world and cunning, though it worked more slowly, was the more reliable. (186)

Recognizing as he does that he is a trimmer, Jon is uncomfortable when faced with Mike and his quixotic passion for the right. "There was a just perceptible curl to Mike's smile. Had he penetrated my mask of sardonic self-assurance, and perceived the timid, cautious soul beneath?" (151)

The foiling of these two men prepares us for some change in their relative positions. This is what results from Jon's crisis of faith; remember that it is precipitated by Pauline's pregnancy, which is caused by the impulsive destruction of the condoms (the mark of the prudent man) which would have prevented it. This act concludes the main narrative, so we know it is important. Why did Jon do it? Here is the passage: "Before taking a seat in the restaurant car, I went to the W.C. and flushed Henry's parting gift down the plug" (206). We can draw one conclusion, though; that flushing is a Michael Brady act, not a Jonathan Browne one. If it is only impulsive and risk-taking, then it is already alien to Jon's temperament; but it is more: it is a repudiation of contraception. One of Mike's poems remembered by Jon reads (rather preposterously)

> It's not the harlot's cry,
> But the contraceptive sheath
> From street to street
> Will weave old England's winding sheet;
> The rubber gloves of prudent lechery
> Leave no traces
> Rifling the virgin's bottom drawer . . .(45)

Thus the repudiation of contraception is, in some measure, a tribute to Mike and perhaps even a partial adoption of his faith. For Catholicism is important in this novel. Mike Brady comes from a large Catholic family

30

with a devout mother and a more easy-going father, like the Mallorys in *The Picturegoers*. Pauline's difficulties with the family, their bristling suspicion of non-Catholics, Mike's insistence on her conversion, provide a glimpse of the practical consequences of Catholicism. Pauline's vexation over the complexity of Catholic doctrine and her frustration because the Bradys *talk* about religion all the time, though, help to brand her as ignorant and spiritually lightweight like Jon. She likes the Church of England because it is convenient and makes few demands: she matches Jon's own prudence and shallowness.

It is fitting, then, that Jon's growth involves at least an ambiguous movement towards Roman Catholicism, just as it requires that he abandon the easy path toward an equivocal success he has been following. He must embrace some of Mike's values, and the Epilogue shows that he has done so. Now his old aims—the settled career, the marriage to Pauline with children to follow—sour, and he faces

> a certain panic when I reflect that he will no longer need my support [because he is being released from prison]. It is not a question of what he will do without me, but of what I will do without him. Now he is free, and I am shackled, —by a wife and family I do not greatly love, and by a career that I find no more than tolerable. (210)

I earlier compared this novel to *Heart of Darkness* and *The Great Gatsby*—at that time thinking mostly of the narrative technique. The conclusion is similar to those as well: the narrator ends by endorsing a character from whom he has held off, on moral grounds. These are impressive comparisons; but how good is *Ginger, You're Barmy?*

I want to answer in two parts. First, as to the treatment of National Service and the fifties. As a document, a social history, a chapter in the moral history of his nation, Lodge's book is successful. As far as I can tell, the verisimilitude of the National Service scenes is adroit; the feeling of reality is very strong. Thomas P. McDonnell, in a strong review of the book written on its American appearance, praised this aspect of the book with a comparison that must have pleased the author:

> Now I should not be so downright insane as to place David Lodge's second novel against what seems to be the final achievement in fiction of Evelyn Waugh, but I would maintain that *Ginger, You're Barmy* is the British army in ways that Waugh's officers and gentlemen are not. [249]

After all, most armies are at peace most of the time; most of the things they do are essentially undramatic, dull, vitiating, and pointless; the lesson of *Ginger, You're Barmy* is in part how ordinary army life is — ordinary while remaining a vicious assault on human dignity.

The book also contains, along with its gritty realism, a certain amount of humor. There is some fun in the figure of Norman, the East Midlands Caliban who ends up as the squadron's pigherd, and in jokes (very likely old Army chestnuts) about the shepherd's pie made from real shepherds. More ambitious is a Kingsley Amis tone which comes into the scenes set at the end of Jon's army days; here is a little gem worth comparing to Professor Welch's driving.

> "Here comes the Captain," said Mr. Fry, folding up his newspaper.
>
> We gathered at the window. It was always worth watching Captain Pirie's arrival, on the off-chance of his hitting something expensive.
>
> The green vintage Bentley swept into the camp in a fast four-wheel drift, passed behind a long row of buildings, and, after a strangely long interval, emerged at the other end going slowly, and disconcertingly, backwards.
>
> "Must've 'it an oil-patch," observed Ludlow knowledgeably.
>
> After much audible wrestling with the gears Captain Pirie pointed the car in our direction and drove furiously towards us, clinging to the great, string-bound steering wheel, and peering myopically through the yellowing windscreen. He swung into the parking bay outside the office, and drew up, missing the Adjutant's Jaguar by inches. (70)

But the other part of the novel which must be judged is more important than its documentary or humorous qualities: the examination of the moral issues affecting Jonathan Browne and Mike Brady. The novel pretty clearly endorses Mike Brady and insists that we recognize, even more strongly than he sometimes perceives himself, that Jonathan Browne's prudence, his avoidance of risks, his ready acceptance of the easy way to a worldly comfort, make him worse than the unreliable and violent Mike Brady, who is at least committed to something.

Jon reflects that "National Service was like a very long, very tedious journey on the Inner Circle" and that "as you approached your destination, you should try to connect the end of your journey with the beginning" (191), and these lines point to both Eliot's *Four Quartets* and the circles of Dante's *Inferno*. Dante put the indecisive outside the vestibule of Hell; having been neither good nor bad, they were left in Limbo after death. And Eliot insists, in a number of places, that it is necessary to be good, or even to be bad, rather than to be nothing. The sinner is not so culpable as the hollow man. In these terms, Jonathan Browne is, until his conversion at the end, a hollow man, distinguished from "violent souls" like Kurtz and Michael Brady, by never having really lived.

That this is the theme of the novel's dialectic between Jon and Mike I have no real doubt. It requires a great deal of Mike Brady, and I believe that Lodge has failed to make a Brady which can bear the moral weight required by this scheme. For one thing, Brady must be drawn clearly. Thomas McDonnell, in an otherwise perceptive review, demonstrates that he has missed the ambivalences in both Mike and Jon, as he sums up the three main characters (Percy Higgins is the first):

> the delicately-balanced who, more precipitously than not, shall be broken by the system; the manic-unbalanced, who wants no other way but violently out; and the finely-balanced, who shall at last not only survive the ordeal but turn it to some new awareness of life itself. (250)

McDonnell misses the lightweight quality, the fear of commitment and the absence of passion which are built into Jonathan Browne's finely balanced nature. And he is further afield on Mike Brady, who (unless I am misreading this book) is not so much manic-unbalanced as quixotically committed to *not* giving up his soul to gain the world. The shape of the novel endorses this evaluation of Mike; so do the the self-criticisms of himself woven into Jonathan's discourse. In the Prologue he writes

> If I take any credit at all, if I think any better of myself now, than I now think of myself *then* — as I portray myself in these pages — it is because I think I have realized that a deterministic conception of character and individual destiny is the subtlest of temptations that dissuade a man conscious of his own defects and others' needs from doing anything about them. I don't think I am a better person, or even a happier one; but perhaps there has been a small advance. I could never again write so unflattering an account of myself as the following, because it would open up so many awful possibilities of amendment. The whole story reeks of a curiously inverted, inviol-

able conceit.

Is that last part not a warning to us readers that we should not take Jonathan as the finely-balanced norm? And the rejection of a deterministic view of character and individual destiny comes from a man who earlier thought that "all human activity was useless," but now agrees with Mike's explanation that he was put on earth "to exercise my free will, and to save my soul" (150). I see no alternative to reading the book as Jonathan Browne's saving his rather brown soul by what he learns from Mike Brady, and rejecting the devil, the world and the flesh in the process. The problem in this scheme is that Mike Brady isn't up to the demands of the role. He can't generate, in the reader, the sympathy and admiration which Jon feels for him.

Partly this is because his cause is only obscurely worthy of our admiration; that is, Percy Higgins has been cruelly treated by Corporal Baker, but the mistreatment did not cause his death; instead it was caused by Percy's incompetent attempt to disable himself for service by following an idea tossed off as a joke by Mike himself. Likewise when, having escaped the army, Mike joins the IRA, it is difficult to see this as a morally superior path; he later expresses some unease about it, and acknowledges that it's "Funny really: out of one Army and into another. There's not much to choose between them, I can tell you" (203). If we cannot think of IRA membership as an almost neutral alternative to the British Army, that is perhaps because the bloody events of the seventies and eighties have changed what the IRA means to readers.

Now perhaps we are not meant to admire Mike's choice of actions, but just the fact that he chose and that he resisted the soul-deadening Army, rather than dying like Percy or collaborating like Jon. Jon thinks that Mike is barmy, and he is apparently the subject of the title and the little song which says "Ginger, you're barmy,/You'll never join the army." And he never does. But his barminess, which is expressed in other ways as well — unconventional dress and haircut, failure to study hard at University, insufficient excitement over his girlfriend — is not enough to make him the polar character towards whom both Jon and the reader must warp.

One more point: this is the only one of David Lodge's novels which is narrated by one of the characters. That it is written in this way seems partly a debt to the models (Graham Greene's *The Quiet American*, by the author's account, and Joseph Conrad by mine), and partly an effort to make the moral lines clear while preserving the reticence and ambiguity which omniscience would dispel. In this the novel succeeds only too well.

34

Chapter Five

LIFE AND ART
THE BRITISH MUSEUM IS FALLING DOWN

Life was transparent, literature opaque. Life was an open, literature a
closed system. Life was composed of things, literature of words.
— Morris Zapp, *Changing Places*

David Lodge's first three books show a curious little pattern in their
relationship to the real-life backgrounds on which they are based. His
undergraduate career at University College London ended in 1955; five
years later *The Picturegoers* placed at its center an undergraduate reading
English at that university. From 1955 to 1957 he was in the army; in 1962
Ginger, You're Barmy used that experience as background. In 1959 he
completed his postgraduate study in English, and in that year and the next
he looked for an academic post; *The British Museum is Falling Down*, about
a postgraduate student trying to finish his thesis and worrying about a
teaching position, appeared in 1965. The facile conclusion, that David
Lodge's novels are about what he was doing five years earlier, will be
dispelled by the next novel, but it does indicate the orderly way in which
he discovers in his own experiences the suitable universality to serve as the
background for an invented plot.

In a number of ways this novel is a departure for Lodge. It is his first
novel set in academic life; it is his first *comic novel*, despite the moments
of comedy in the first two books; and it is the first to use playfulness,
self-consciousness and literary parody in a deliberate movement away
from traditional realism. In an introduction written in 1981 the author
explained:

> My first two books, *The Picturegoers* and *Ginger, You're Barmy*, had
> had their moments of humour, but both were essentially works of
> scrupulous realism. Through the experience of working on *Between
> These Four Walls* [a satirical revue of which he was one co-author],
> I discovered in myself a zest for satirical, farcical and parodic
> writing that I had not known I possessed; and this liberated me, I
> found, from the restrictive decorums of the well-made, realistic
> novel. *The British Museum is Falling Down* was the first of my novels
> that could be described as in any way experimental. Comedy, it

35

seemed, offered a way of reconciling a contradiction, of which I had long been aware, between my critical admiration of the great modernist writers, and my creative practice, formed by the neo-realist, antimodernist writing of the 1950s. (BM 6)

There are a number of discoveries here which helped to liberate Lodge. One is the use of the antihero, or at least the perfectly ordinary man at the center of his fiction. This not only permits comic misadventures but allays some of the tension which is detectable in the development of Mike Brady in *Ginger*. Another advance is the incorporation of the author's literary, and even literary-critical, knowledge fully into the text. In the past it had hovered: Mark Underwood and Jonathan Browne, students in English literature, introduced a certain number of literary references. But Adam Appleby, a postgraduate student in English who is moreover preoccupied with his subject, allows for a novel steeped in English literature. The obvious danger of this course—pretentiousness—is avoided by having Adam the victim, rather than the showy wielder, of his literary knowledge.

The plot of *The British Museum is Falling Down* is episodic. It follows Adam through the tumultuous events of one day in his life, a day made special by his agonizing worry that his wife may be pregnant again (with their fourth child); his other major worry, about the completion of his thesis and his academic future, is rather less special, though made more pointed on this day by his failure to do any academic work and the special practical and financial crisis which another child would precipitate. During the day Adam spends time in the British Museum, though he never buckles down to work; he talks with his friend Camel; he calls Barbara to see if her period has started; he accidentally raises a fire alarm in the British Museum reading room; he attends a faculty–student sherry, where he gets, then loses, a teaching position for the following year; he discovers a valuable literary manuscript, which would make his career, but realizes that he must sleep with a teenage girl to obtain it; he tries to buy contraceptives but is foiled by the inopportune arrival of his parish priest; he obtains the manuscript without bedding the girl, but loses it when his scooter explodes and burns; he is offered a part-time job by an American whom he has run into repeatedly all day; finally he goes home and goes to sleep, while his wife, whose period has started, has the last word in the novel.

As Lodge has acknowledged, the basic model for this novel is *Ulysses*, at least insofar as it follows one protagonist through a day's wanderings; Adam, like Bloom, thinks of his wife all day and at the end of it returns to her. And the Epilogue of the novel, given to us in Barbara's thoughts, is

36

based on Molly's soliloquy in the Penelope chapter of *Ulysses*, and parodies it fairly closely.

This novel revolves on two binary oppositions, or dialectical relationships. One of them, akin to the antithesis of army and civilian life in *Ginger*, is that between Adam's home life and his intellectual work at the Museum. As he tries to assure himself when he seems to glimpse his family, briefly, through the fog, at the British Museum itself:

> It *was* a dream, of course. Although the Museum was notoriously a place where eventually you met everyone you knew, this law did not include dependents. Scholarship and domesticity were opposed worlds, whose common frontier was marked by the Museum railings. (105)

This comforting certitude is of course false, for not only are Barbara and the three children actually in the Museum (though Adam never encounters them), but his thoughts have been on domestic matters the whole day and he has frequently phoned home to inquire about them.

The other far more important dualism opposes art and life. We may even say that this is what the novel is about. Adam has given thought to this problem, as well, and sometimes is convinced that the two are different. Observing the way Adam's life falls into literary patterns, his friend claims that Adam is "no longer able to distinguish between life and literature," to which he responds, "Oh yes I can . . . Literature is mostly about having sex and not much about having children. Life is the other way round". (63)

This distinction aside, though, Adam is uneasily aware of the inter-penetration of life and literature in his own case. Throughout the day, under the special pressure of his worries, he lapses into reveries or daydreams in which his life takes on the characteristics of the literature of one of the modern novelists on whom he is supposedly writing a thesis. And, as he is studying "The Structure of Long Sentences in Three Modern English Novels," these scenes are narrated in a parodic form of the language of the novelists, fueled by Adam's familiarity with their styles. I will deal with the function and quality of these parodies later, but the important point for now is that they represent, in a dramatic way, the collapse of the distinction (which was of course never really absolute) between art and life. This collapse takes place, in terms of psychological realism, in Adam's mind (though Barbara's epilogue is autonomous — and anomalous), and is motivated by psychological disturbance; but it also illustrates a point which Adam makes, when drunk at the sherry party.

Responding to a bald-headed man who keeps asking his opinion of English writers Kingsley Anus, C. P. Slow, and John Bane, he explains his theory that "novelists are *using up* experience at a dangerous rate," since novels, unlike romances, concentrate on ordinary life. The result is that

> there've been such a fantastic number of novels written in the last couple of centuries that they've just about exhausted the pos-sibilities of life. So all of us, you see, are really enacting events that have already been written about in some novel or other. Of course, most people don't realize this — they fondly imagine that their little lives are unique . . . . Just as well, too, because when you *do* tumble to it, the effect is very disturbing. (130)

At first glance we may see Adam as anticipating the famous claims advanced in John Barth's 1967 essay on postmodern fiction, "The Litera-ture of Exhaustion." But in fact Adam and Barth have two different kinds of exhaustion in mind; Barth is concerned with the exhaustion, by earlier writers, of all literary possibilities, and he concludes, with Borges, that "for one to attempt to add overtly to the sum of 'original' literature by even so much as a conventional short story, not to mention a novel, would be too presumptuous, too naive; literature has been done long since" (Barth 80). Barth is pointing out how hard it is to *write* without echoing a predecessor, a phenomenon which Lodge calls "belatedness" and defines as follows: "the awareness every young writer has of the daunting weight of literary tradition, and the necessity, yet seeming impossibility, of doing something in writing that has not been done already" (WO 66). Adam Appleby is actually making a bolder claim: the accumulation of literary precedents has made it impossible to *live* originally, to do something *in one's life* that has not been done already in someone's book. Of course, since Adam is really a fictional character in a book which reuses its predecessors, there is another Barthian dimension, understood by David Lodge but not by Adam Appleby, to this theory.

To say that this novel is about the relationship between art and life is another way of saying that its subject is realism. In this way, too, it conflates David Lodge's critical interests with his activities as a novelist, since he has given particular attention to the claims of realism and the objections against it. In his early critical work, as in his early fiction, he wrote strongly in defense of realism: for instance, in this lucid explanation, found in *Language of Fiction* (1966):

The circumstantial particularity of the novel is thus a kind of anti-convention. It attempts to disguise the fact that a novel is discontinuous with real life. It suggest that the life of a novel is a bit of real life which we happen not to have heard about before, but which somewhere is or was going on. The novelist peoples the world of verifiable data (Dublin, a seaport, capital of Ireland, contains a street called Eccles St) with fictitious characters and events (Leopold Bloom, Jew, advertising salesman, married, one daughter living, one son dead, is cuckolded, befriends a young man). The novelist moves cautiously from the real to the fictional world, and takes pains to conceal the movement. (LF 42)

Though this book and *The British Museum is Falling Down* are nearly contemporaneous in date of publication (and Adam Appleby's thesis topic, a linguistic analysis of three modern novels, may nod slyly at Lodge's own work), the novel in fact incorporates some of the dubiety about the centrality of realism which Lodge gets around to discussing in his next critical work, *The Novelist at the Crossroads* (published in 1971). The crossroads represents the *huis clos* of traditional realism and the choice between "fabulation" and the "nonfiction novel." *The British Museum* has some of this crossroads feeling, as well; it is both realism and fabulation, both modernist and postmodernist.

In one way even the extensive and conspicuous parodies in the text do not puncture the realistic skin; after all, they are given to us as part of the mental activity of Adam Appleby. We might contrast the "Oxen of the Sun" chapter of *Ulysses*, in which Joyce recapitulates in pastiche form the development of English prose. It is far more ambitious than Lodge's project in *The British Museum*; and it is different, too, in not being focalized through one of the characters. It is difficult to say precisely what the ontology of Joyce's parodies is. They certainly are not the mental property of any of the novel's characters, and thus are a reminder of the author's looming presence. They are metafictional. Lodge's parodies are within the fiction, anchored to the minds of the characters. "All this," as Robert Burden insists, "is consistent with the novel's fundamental realism; Adam's obsessive fantasizing is made plausible from the very outset" (141).

Given this justification — the parodies belong here because they are the kind of thing which would occupy the troubled mind of an Adam Appleby — we may ask if they are justified in another sense: do they add anything to the novel? Are they any good? And the answer to both of these questions is yes. They add, first of all, amusement. This is a comic novel; in addition to a level of comedy which is fundamental and unsubtle — Adam's scooter exploding, a funny conversation at cross-purposes with Father Finbar in the contraceptive shop, the discovery, as Adam is threatened almost with rape by a predatory teenager, that he is wearing his wife's lacy underthings — there is a literary comedy provided by the parodies. Rather than having Adam simply drift off into parodied reveries, Lodge has placed them very appropriately. Adam has to thread the hallways of the Museum to renew his reader's ticket, and his worry converts this experience into something out of Kafka. Confronted by mysterious Easterners (Marxist pilgrims from the People's Republic of China, as it happens) Adam works up a steamy moment of moral crisis in the Conradian vein. The best of the parodies occurs when Adam is negotiating with a Mrs. Rottingdean for some unpublished materials by Catholic writer Egbert Merrymarsh. The situation is fraught and Lodge renders it in a good pastiche of Henry James. Here is how it begins:

> It was with a, for him, unwonted alacrity that our friend, hearing the tinkle of china in the hall, sprang gallantly to the door.
> "I've been admiring your 'things'," he said, as he assisted her with the tea-trolley.(115)

Characteristically Jamesian evasions and circumlocutions and odd turns of syntax, peppered with irrelevant quotation marks, continue. This passage of analysis rings very true:

> The memory of Merrymarsh was evidently a tender one, and it seemed as though the question of manuscripts would have to be delicately broached. He fairly rattled the small change of conversation in his pocket without lighting on a single coin that wouldn't, in the circumstances, seem too soiled and worn, too vulgarly confident of being "hard" currency. (116)

James is notoriously hard to parody, and Lodge does him well. The parody of Hemingway is not as good. In general, though, the quality of the parodies is high. Probably the best one is that contained in the Epilogue, in which Barbara's thoughts follow those of Molly Bloom, lying in bed, thinking over her husband's return and his account of his day. Like Molly, Barbara has begun her period; this is what Adam has hoped for all day, though he is asleep and doesn't know it. Like Molly, Barbara thinks back over her courtship, and this part of the Epilogue, the conclusion, is the

40

section of this book where the parody proves itself most worthwhile. Barbara ends with these words:

> ... you're not very optimistic, he said perhaps it's better not to be, I said I'm going to be famous and earn lots of money, he said perhaps you won't love me then, I said I'll always love you, he said I'll prove it every night he kissed my throat perhaps you think that now I said but I couldn't keep it up perhaps we will be happy, I said of course we will, he said, we'll have a nanny to look after the children perhaps we will, I said, by the way how many children are we going to have as many as you like, he said it'll be wonderful you'll see perhaps it will, I said perhaps it will be wonderful perhaps even though it won't be like you think perhaps that won't matter perhaps. (175-76)

This is really beautiful; the shift from Adam's humorous fantasizing to the more realistic Barbara, the ironic view of several of the novel's themes, particularly sex and children, and the tentative conclusion provided by substituting *perhaps* for Molly's *yes*. All these testify to the seriousness of this novel, to the fact that comedy need not be frivolous – and to the underlying realism, for after all Barbara's is the voice of realism, in this memory, punctuating Adam's romantic fantasies of the future.

Though there is no ready explanation why Barbara's thoughts should be a close parody of Molly Bloom's soliloquy – Barbara is not working on the sentence structure of modern novels, and this is not a fantasy – still the novel keeps one foot in the realist camp.

In the realist mode it provides the kind of telling detail on its subjects which we have come to expect from Lodge's earlier books. This is the first of Lodge's novels to give central place to both Catholicism and the academic community. Adam's twin problems derive from these two worlds: his wife's possible pregnancy, and in a larger sense, the difficulty of avoiding conception, are specifically Catholic problems; his failure to thrive as a scholar, his poverty and uncertain prospects, are academic woes. This novel gives us *sketches* of the academy rather than the full picture of university life which some academic novels provide. There are several reasons for this; as a postgraduate student, Adam is marginal, neither undergraduate nor lecturer. Writing a thesis is lonely work, linked to no system of benchmarks or rewards, softened only by sharing the misery with others in the same predicament. Adam's academic contacts are almost exclusively with his friends who work in the British Museum. Like

41

him, they demonstrate the difficulty of finishing the thesis; one of them, Camel, is famous for his interminable work on Sanitation in Victorian Fiction, a project which ramifies endlessly.

Another fact of Adam's kind of life is the infrequent and impersonal contact with the English faculty. An exception is the sherry party; there, Adam is to be given a teaching post for the next year, but it goes to Camel instead because the Head of English cannot tell them apart. There is a bit of donnish feuding over chairs and some more over office assignments. It is funny, not very penetrating, and certainly not savage.

The focus on Catholicism is, as we often find with Lodge, on the practical rather than theological side, and particularly on matters of sex and reproduction. The most important fact of the novel is Barbara's possible pregnancy. Adam's melancholy reflections on the unreliability of the rhythm method, on the annoyance and anti-aphrodisiac effects of Barbara's temperature-taking and graph-making, and his envy of more fortunate non-Catholics ostensibly enjoying wild uninhibited sex lives: all these provide further comment on the effects of Rome's doctrine on the prevention of conception.

But if these are the reports from the realist camp, there is another side to *The British Museum is Falling Down*: the side which we may call metafictional or self-conscious. Though this aspect is less fully developed than it will be in such later books as *Changing Places* and *Small World*, it is, for the first time in Lodge's work, an emphatically developed part of the novel. By "self-conscious," I mean, in Robert Alter's definition,

> a novel that systematically flaunts its own condition of artifice and that by so doing probes into the problematic relationship between real-seeming artifice and reality. I would lay equal stress on the ostentatious nature of the artifice and the systematic nature of the flaunting. (x-xi)

Bernard Bergonzi refers to the same phenomenon in *The Situation of the Novel*: the novels he discusses, including *The British Museum is Falling Down*,

> are all examples of what Wells called "the frame getting into the picture," where the author's act of writing is included in the field of the novel. By their shuffling of levels of reality, their reliance on collage and pastiche and parody, they point to possible redefinitions of the novel, in which, as I have suggested, the distinction

between fiction and other kinds of writing could become blurred. (210)

Bergonzi insists that these novels are parasitic on the realistic novel, because their parodies depend on it. Lodge's in particular is what Alter would call a partly self-conscious novel, one with "isolated pockets or fits and starts of fictional self-consciousness in a novel that is for the most part conventionally realistic" (xi). The parodies call attention to themselves, to the fictional process and to the fiction-maker. They are, thus, partial disruptions of the realistic pattern still predominant in this book.

More clearly self-conscious than the moments of parody—for these, after all, have a "naturalistic" explanation in terms of Adam's psychology—more openly disruptive of the realistic surface, are the moments when the novel comments on itself. Early on, after Adam has met an American named Bernie Schnitz, he tells his friend Camel: "If I was the hero of one of these comic novels . . . he would be the fairy-godfather who would turn up at the end to offer me a job and a girl" (82). This remark glances particularly, I think, at Amis's (or Anus's) *Lucky Jim*, where Gore-Urquhart by offering Jim a job solves all his problems: a romantic conclusion indeed. We know, as we read Adam Appleby's words, that he actually is the hero of a comic novel, and we probably are not very surprised, then, when Bernie Schnitz becomes his fairy-godfather, offering him a job which alleviates some of his financial needs.

Similarly we learn from Barbara's bedtime reflections in the Epilogue that Adam is "always in a dream, what was it he said, a novel where life kept taking the shape of literature, did you ever hear anything so cracked, life is life and books are books and if he was a woman he wouldn't need to be told that" (172). In other words, Adam has thought up the idea for *The British Museum is Falling Down*. When we think back to the rather categorical declaration Lodge makes in *Language of Fiction*, that "the novelist moves cautiously from the real to the fictional world, and takes pains to conceal the movement" (42) we realize that Lodge's idea of what "the novel" does has changed quite a lot. Now the novelist moves between the real and the fictional worlds and not only fails to conceal the movement but flaunts it. This is a grand playfulness about the problem of reality in the novel. This theme, and the sharply adjusted novelistic method which accompanies it—and even the newly discovered ability to write comedy and farce which also accompanies it—are the most important features of David Lodge's best novels, which are still to come.

But first, a step backward.

43

Chapter Six

BACK INTO THE SHELTER
OUT OF THE SHELTER

In *Out of the Shelter* (1970), Lodge looks backward in every way. For the first time he has written a fully retrospective novel; that is to say, though all his novels are set in the past (as are almost all novels, of course), usually it is the quite recent past in Lodge's experience which provides the milieu for the fictional events of the book. As I have noted, there is a roughly five-year gap between the living and the writing. For example, *The British Museum is Falling Down* (1965) is played out against a background of postgraduate study, which Lodge completed in 1959.

Now he goes back all the way to childhood. *Out of the Shelter* examines two important periods in the life of Timothy Young; the first one is his fifth year, during the Blitz, when he first encounters death. After some bridging material covering his growing and schooling, the greater part of the novel is set in 1951, when Timothy is sixteen.

The novel is retrospective in another way. It reverts to the type of fiction Lodge was writing before his discovery, in *British Museum*, of his gifts for playfulness, comedy, and self-consciousness. As usual, the author's explanation is enlightening.

> *Out of the Shelter* (1970) was the fourth of my novels to be published, coming between *The British Museum is Falling Down* and *Changing Places*, but it was conceived before the earlier of those books, and in tone and technique has much more in common with my first two works of fiction, *The Picturegoers* and *Ginger, You're Barmy*. That is to say, it is a "serious" realistic novel in which comedy is an incidental rather than a structural element, and metafictional games and stylistic experiment are not allowed to disturb the illusion of life. (278)

It is also his most autobiographical novel. One feels that David Lodge believes (as the grown-up Timothy tells his sister in the Epilogue) "There's a gap opening up, getting wider all the time, between those who remember the war, rationing, austerity, and so on, and those who were too young to remember, or born afterwards" (264). *Out of the Shelter* seems designed — in part, but it is an important part of the design — to bear witness to those vanished days. The story of the war years is told naively, impressionistically, with the limitations of understanding and expression natural to a five year old boy, so it would be unrealistic to expect documentary accuracy or comprehensiveness in its picture of wartime life. But better than these is the emotional accuracy—or at least emotional persuasiveness—of the early part of the book, which is called *"The Shelter."* This is the best part of the book.

The novel is a *Bildungsroman* focusing on Timothy Young, a lower-middle-class boy from South London. The first section, set in wartime, briefly but effectively sketches in a number of important themes, the most important one being shelter. Timothy and his mother, we learn, are accustomed to share a shelter with a neighboring family consisting of Jill, a little girl his age, her Mummy, and her father whom Timothy calls Uncle Jack. One night there is a raid; Timothy and Jill are put to bed in the shelter (where they fall asleep fondling each other's genitals); awoken by nearby bombing, Jill and her mother leave the shelter to find Uncle Jack and are blown up. Though dazed, Timothy and his mother are safe; when men come to dig them out, "Timothy didn't want to leave the shelter. In the end, one of the men had to carry him, kicking and screaming, out of the shelter, into the open air" (14).

Here the author sets up his carefully symbolic treatment of the shelter. Timothy has to come out of the shelter, of course, but he is also dimly aware that bad things happen when you do. Jill and her mother were killed because they came out of the shelter. The novel will use the idea of emerging from shelter as a metaphor for growing up; but Timothy is of two minds about that, as well; he both wants to emerge from shelter and fears it. Timothy's experience in the shelter also becomes associated with sexuality, since he and Jill were touching each other sexually just before she was killed. Timothy associates sex with punishment for a long time— that is, until he comes out of the shelter sexually. Throughout the novel various shelters will present themselves; sometimes these are literal, as when the adolescent Timothy, vacationing with his parents at the seaside, finds a Corporation shelter at the end of the Promenade: "Alone in the shelter, under cover of night, safe from observation, Timothy lapsed into a heroic dream of his childhood" (52). Other shelters are metaphorical, such as the choice of an undemanding job doing architectural drawings which his father urges on him as an alternative to the unknown and thus frightening possibility of going to university.

Along with the summary treatment of Timothy's life between age five and sixteen there are occasional reports on his sister Kate. Much older,

45

she had been at convent school during the war; after school she joined the Americans as a secretary and moved to liberated Paris, then to postwar Heidelberg. She visits very rarely, bringing loads of good things — cigarettes, food, stockings — which dazzle her privation-dulled family. She is unhappy at home and gets along poorly with her mother, and finally, after a long period without a visit, she invites Timothy to join her for a holiday in Heidelberg. Her invitation brings the main action of the book. It brings Timothy out of the shelter.

The eventful few weeks in Heidelberg are for him a rite of passage, a threshold experience between childhood and maturity. Timothy learns important lessons about four things: Kate, sex, the Germans, and the Americans.

The lesson about Kate is tied up with Timothy's Catholicism and his provincialism. He has never really known Kate well — as we have seen, the five-year-old Timothy is already separated from her by her removal from London — and she is, for him, a mystery. For a time she is a mystery of awkwardness and ugliness: Kate is always fat and, the family unreflectingly assumes, unattractive. Later, after she begins working for the Americans, she is a mystery of luxury and privilege. Her infrequent letters give a glimpse of plentiful money and frequent travel to exotic locations. And her unwillingness to come back home (quite understandable, really, once we see the contrast between her pinched home and her life in Heidelberg) can only be interpreted by the Young family as evidence of sin. Timothy overhears his mother speculating on Kate and suggesting that she is afraid to return because she is no longer "a decent Catholic girl" (48), and this explanation seems plausible to him. He imagines a scene in which Kate will introduce him to her bastard daughter. He also expects her to behave like a sinner. To his surprise, though she no longer attends Mass, she is casual rather than lurid about it; when he finally reveals his thoughts about her infamy she explains that she is a virgin.

Timothy's conversation with Kate helps him to give her a real human status for him; they talk about her and their parents and, for the first time, she becomes something more than a mystery or caricature. Timothy moves in her direction, inadvertently eating meat on Friday. Kate loses her long-preserved virginity, with a man to whom Timothy has introduced her. By this time his own opinions about faith and sex have been complicated so that his judgments are no longer so absolute.

For Timothy, discovering sex is almost summed up in the discovery that girls have pubic hair. For him, adolescent sexuality is largely voyeurism, as he and his friends scan not-very-revealing photos, and "the limit of his sexual ambition had been to see a grown-up girl bare, like he had seen Jill. To see the part that was always hidden, somehow, in paintings, or photographs, like the ones in *Razzle*" (50). He does this much and more in Heidelberg. First, staying illicitly in a woman's hostel, he hears the woman next door in the act of sex, even using obscene language. He can hear her because he has entered a wardrobe in his room which is against her wall, described, significantly, as "a shelter within a shelter" (116). Later he accidentally locks himself in it; the woman — whose rather unlikely name is Jinx Dobell — has to help him out. As she has literally released him from the shelter, she offers herself to him, in a symbolic unsheltering, but he is repelled by what he sees: "Not the smooth, pearl-pink little dimpled cleft of his mind's eye, but hair, a beard of vivid ginger hair, dense and wiry as a fox's tail, shadowing vertical lips of loose, brownish skin" (198). It surprises and repels him.

He is soon able to accomodate himself to his discovery, which finally proves liberating rather than inhibiting, when he sees his sister Kate and his friend Don, now lovers, lying naked together. He reflects:

> He had been shocked when he saw it on the Jinx woman, but seeing it again on Kate he hadn't been shocked. It made women seem more like men. . . . There had been something beautiful about Kate and Don lying on the bed, but that was taking all of their bodies together. Taken all together they had looked rather beautiful, like a painting. Though all the paintings, and the photographs, he had seen of naked women had been deeply misleading. (209)

Having gone beyond both his earlier sensational ideas about sex and damnation and his unrealistic expectations of women as hairless angels, Timothy is now ready for his own sexual initiation. It occurs when he joins a young people's party on a boat, overcomes his shyness to talk to a girl named Gloria Rose, and succeeds in getting her back to his hostel room the next afternoon. Undeterred by pubic hair or even the threats of hell, he gets her clothes off and they pet to orgasm. (It is true that Timothy immediately makes plans to go to confession on the morrow.)

In the conversation which follows Gloria reveals that, though she stops short of intercourse in fear of pregnancy, she enjoys this sort of sex—just because it's fun. As for sinfulness, she is of vague religious background and heedless of any moral arguments against indulgence. She is clearly a hedonist, telling Timothy that "that's what it's all about, between guys and girls. To feel and not think" (244). Their argument, in which Timothy defends thinking, and even worrying, is clearly meant to be part of the ongoing contrast between the English and the Americans which is more fully developed in the persons of Kate's American friends.

It is a mark of Lodge's control, I believe, that he does not give Timothy the complete sexual success which is a feature, and a very unconvincing one, of so many adolescent-coming-of-age stories. Timothy's experiences with Gloria are already so far beyond what he (and perhaps we) expect, his sexual maturing—maturity in understanding, I mean, as he was physically mature before—so rapid and easy as to strain at the bounds of plausibility. Timothy is, by the way, the only one of Lodge's Catholic protagonists who never worries about contraception. With Gloria he wishes to make love without thinking of the consequences (a notion she ridicules); in the Epilogue we find that the adult Timothy, though still a Catholic, is married to a non-Catholic and doesn't object to her using birth control. Apparently he has developed into a liberal Catholic like those Lodge portrays in *How Far Can You Go?*

The third area in which Timothy must learn is in his attitude to the Germans. The change here is towards complexity, away from absolutism. Quite understandably, given his experience of the Blitz, the death of all of Jill's family by German action, the privations of the war, and the wartime propaganda at an impressionable age, Timothy knows invincibly how demonic the Germans are. At about seven, he thinks

> Hitler was the head of the Germans. He had started the war. He was a nasty man with a black moustache. Another name for Germans was Nazis, which sounded like Nasties, so it was a good name. (20)

He hates the Germans for killing Uncle Jack, a tail-gunner in a bomber, and the discovery of the horrors of Belsen after the German defeat gives him a sort of satisfaction:

> Timothy felt almost glad—glad that the Germans had been shown to be wicked beyond all imagining, for it confirmed the righteousness of the war. It was as if all the evil and nastiness and cruelty in the world had been drawn into one place and was now being punished and stamped out, crushed between the mighty armies of the Allies. (29)

This sort of heightened emotion makes his visit to Heidelberg a problematic undertaking. Though now crushed by the Allies, the Germans might still retain their nastiness and evil and cruelty.

Timothy's views change when he learns that the Germans are, after all, ordinary people like him and, more troublingly, when he learns that the Allies did horrible things to the Germans as well. Only once does the demonic Germany of his imagination appear: climbing the street he sees a man drinking water.

> Then, as he approached, the man straightened up, and turned to face Timothy, wiping his mouth with the back of his hand. It was a face of such coarse brutality that, in spite of the warm day, Timothy turned cold with fear. A bumpy, shaven iron-grey skull, small bloodshot eyes, flared nostrils, thick lips elongated into a sneer by a scar that curved down to the jawline – he took in this much as he swerved aside and stumbled on up the hill. (128)

This incident aside – and it is only in the melodramatic imagination of an adolescent that physical ugliness guarantees moral evil – nothing in Germany answers to Timothy's dark expectations. The German people are, mostly, invisible beneath the glossy surface of the American occupation; when they become visible they turn out to be about like the English. Timothy's friendship with Rudolf, a young German who works in his sister's hostel, helps him to perceive German humanity; his experience of Rudolf's family, including a father who has been blacklisted for ambiguous implication in Nazi activities, complicates and unsettles his certitude about the responsibility for evil. Now he sees that some Germans were victims of the war, too. Rudolf, for instance, has lost an arm and was a prisoner of war in England, while his father is unable to find work, even while outright Nazis of greater value to the occupiers are "deNazified."

The other important impulse in changing Timothy's attitude to the Germans is his dawning realization that all the wrong was not on one side. His friend Don, who was a conscientious objector during the war and is some sort of leftist activist in 1951, helps him by showing him the bomb damage in Frankfurt and informing him that the Dresden raid killed 130,000 civilians compared to the 13,000 victims of the Blitz. At no time are the Allies shown to be morally indistinguishable from the Nazis, but their claims to represent unalloyed good against evil cannot withstand the evidence which Timothy reluctantly takes in. This is, of course, another stage in his passage from childhood to some sort of adulthood. Adults know that wars are not fought between angels and devils. War propaganda succeeds with children and with the childlike in adults. Timothy's new understanding is another sign of maturity.

In the Afterword written for the 1985 reissue of *Out of the Shelter*, David Lodge explained its literary precedents:

> Generically, it is a combination of the *Bildungsroman* (the useful German term for a novel about the passage from childhood to maturity and the recognition of one's vocation) and the Jamesian "international" novel of conflicting ethical and cultural codes. James Joyce's *A Portrait of the Artist as a Young Man* and Henry James's *The Ambassadors* are its most obvious literary models. (275)

Leaving aside for the moment the debt to Joyce, *The Ambassadors* provides a useful entrance into the fourth major thematic node in this novel, Timothy and the Americans. In *The Ambassadors* the American Lambert Strether confronts Europe late in life, enlarges his own imagination and learns, too late, about his failure to live fully. The similarity between this novel and Lodge's would seem to consist largely in this: Strether is "sent" to Paris to bring home a young American who has overstayed himself there and is suspected of having fallen prey to wickedness; Timothy is commissioned by his mother to find out why Kate won't come home, and he goes to Heidelberg prepared for lurid revelations of her fallen state. Both Strether and Timothy have to concede that the person in question has in fact been improved, rather than ruined.

Beyond that, *Out of the Shelter* has a more general Jamesian tone, deriving from its use of the "international theme." As a subject matter for James, this usually involved his putting Americans into contrast (or conflict) with Europeans and Europeanized Americans. The results of the collision of cultures and codes of ethics are often unhappy (e.g. *The American*, *The Portrait of a Lady*, *Daisy Miller*). Lodge does it a little differently. His innocent is an English lad and he is confronted with Americans (and the partly Americanized English, like his sister). The Americans are in some ways more experienced; in others even more innocent.

Here we find the familiar dialectical relationship which we have found to be a fundamental pattern in much of Lodge's fiction: Timothy is English, Catholic, and (as his name implies) timid and young; happiest in shelter; fond of the familiar; naive, romantic, inexperienced. Most of the Americans are carefree, even careless, hedonistic, poorly informed, vulgar, loud, wealthy. They are also emotionally more liberated than Timothy and have much more fun. They are friendly to him, despite his youth, and generous with their money. The two most exemplary Americans are Kate's friends Vince and Greg, who seem to be no more than light-hearted, good-natured playboys. They are free of the uglier traces of xenophobia, anti-Semitism and red-baiting which affect some of their friends. Kate, who is under their spell, explains their attitude to life:

> . . . we have something in common. We want to forget, perhaps that's it. We want to live in the present. We want fun and companionship without emotional involvement, without the risk of getting hurt again. And we do have a lot of fun, you've seen that. (167)

As we have seen, Gloria Rose, Timothy's American sex partner, espouses a similar philosophy. Timothy moves in this direction, as well.

Readers may be prepared for the exposure of the shallow materialism which underlies Vince and Greg's lives, but not for the surprisingly melodramatic form that revelation takes. It turns out that Vince and Greg are not just superficial pleasure-seekers; they are bitter manipulators, who arrange for Don to be fired from his job teaching American dependents; at a party they reveal themselves to be decadent voluptuaries who delight in wearing Nazi uniforms in shocking disregard for the reality of Nazism and the presence of some of its victims; they are homosexuals who have depraved Rudolf and loaned him a car which he smashes up, endangering his life; and they have even attempted to sell American secrets to the East Germans. This all strikes a false, almost hysterial note. The lives of Vince and Greg have already been shown as superficial and hypocritical; must the author overdetermine their punishments quite so spectacularly?

The exposure seems designed primarily to explain why Kate turns against Vince and Greg, once her constant companions. But she doesn't turn against Americans, and in fact carries out her intended emigration. In part her decision reflects the dreariness of English life and the lack of prospects for someone like her. But it is also testimony to another conflict in the book, this time between different types of Americans.

For Vince and Greg are contrasted with, and even to some extent exposed by, another American, Don Kowalski. Don is a poorly-paid teacher; an ex-GI rather than officer material; a conscientious objector to the war; an atheist of Polish-Jewish extraction; thoughtful, left-wing, un-stylish, un-hedonistic, a sort of skull beneath the skin of American self-satisfaction and the life founded on fun.

Chapter Five of the novel, called "Out of the Shelter," begins with a long section in which Timothy, writing a postcard to his parents, relives in flashback his first ten days in Heidelberg. This section is carefully constructed to juxtapose the world of Greg and Vince and their companions with the world of Don. Timothy *enjoys* the former, but is uneasy about its incessant and childish pursuit of pleasure; Don makes him even more uncomfortable, though, by shaking his moral certainties. From time to time the two worlds intersect, as Don tries to befriend Timothy and Kate while their other friends are around; but the disapproval is evident on both sides. Condescension toward Don's ex-GI status, his unorthodox opinions, and his Jewish appearance add to the lack of *bonhomie*. The contrasting scenes work nicely to delineate the contrasting forces in Timothy's mind: Timothy roaring down the highway in Vince's fast car is followed by Timothy receiving Don's advice on education; Vince's fascinated reveling in Hitler lore followed by Don's prescient warnings about Joseph McCarthy; the Vince and Greg gang's riotous life at Baden-Baden followed by Don's sober meditations on Auschwitz.

Don becomes a moral monitor for both Timothy and Kate. Timothy receives frequent lessons from the rather didactic Don on American guilt, the sins of camp-followers like Greg and Vince, and Auschwitz. Kate eventually becomes his lover. The high moment of the novel, emotionally speaking, is the party where the decadent Americans dance in Nazi gear during a fireworks display, clearly a sort of *Götterdämerung*; the narrator tells us that "the guests had conjured an element of genuine evil in the room" (255). Don arrives later, having visited poor Rudolf in the hospital, and pulls the plug on the festivities. He and Kate and Timothy leave together.

Even so, the British/American innocence/experience dialectic is by no means simple. We are left with a lingering admiration for the forward-looking energy of the Americans and a genuine admiration for their abundant living, even some of its material aspects. But the dark underside, perhaps, is a moral blindness best epitomized by Vince and Greg. Don is morally aware, and suspicious of merely material improvements. It must be admitted, though, that Don is a prig.

I have summarized Timothy's growth, his movement out of the shelter, as a process of widening his understanding of people and issues. He must unlearn his simplistic ideas, accustom himself (frustrating as it may be) to complexity and ambiguity. More important, he must learn to see beneath the surface. His encounter with the frightening German leads him to this reflection: "Meeting the ugly man had been like kicking a stone in a summer garden and uncovering a loathsome nest of insects—it made you distrust the smiling surface of things" (128). The reflection makes no sense in this particular case: the man's ugliness is only of the surface, he has not disclosed anything beneath it. But the ability to look past appearances to the deeper reality—an ability which is also a sort of emergence from shelter—*is* one of Timothy's acquisitions from his international initiation.

Finally, in a development which is probably meant to be more important than it in fact seems in the book, Timothy realizes that he does in fact have academic ability: "for the first time in his life he sensed the possibility that he might not be entirely ordinary" (212). He decides to continue at school, aiming for university, rather than go into the apprenticeship his father wants for him. He is partly under the influence of Don, who wants to do postgraduate work at the London School of Economics. Timothy's decision is in accordance with the convention that a *Bildungsroman* leads to the protagonist's discovery of his vocation.

* * * * *

In the Afterword which he wrote for the republication of *Out of the Shelter* in 1985 (presumably stimulated by the success of *Small World* in 1984), David Lodge writes modestly about its earlier obscurity:

> The novel was never paperbacked, or published in America, or translated into another language. It was the least successful of my novels, and is certainly the least well known, though a few of my friends like it more than any of the others.
>
> How far, and in what proportions, this relative neglect of *Out of the Shelter* was due to bad timing, poor production, or the literary quality of the text itself, would be hard to gauge and is, in any case, not for me to say. (281)

In *Write On* (67-68) he has in fact diagnosed some of the shortcomings of this novel, primarily in conjunction with its most obvious model, Joyce's *Portrait*. Now obviously it is no shame to fall short of Joyce. No writer has ever withstood comparison with Joyce on his own ground.

But this would seem to be an urgent reason not to invite that comparison. As we have seen, Lodge makes use of Joyce in *The British Museum is Falling Down*, both by including a pastiche of Molly's monologue in the Epilogue and by a loosely adapted structural similarity in Adam's peregrinations. Even the assemblage of parodies looks toward *Ulysses* and the "Oxen of the Sun." In this novel Lodge played games with the Joycean heritage; reverent games, to be sure, but something other than simple imitation.

In *Out of the Shelter* the relationship to the models is simpler and closer to mere imitation. There is nothing ironic about the relationship between Lodge's novel and Joyce's, as there is in *British Museum*. Instead we notice, for instance, that for the first time Lodge has abandoned quotation marks, or inverted commas, to signal direct speech and substituted the hyphens which Joyce insisted on for *Dubliners* and *A Portrait*. Likewise, the opening, though not as striking as that in which Stephen Dedalus muses on the moocow, uses the same technique of rendering the consciousness of an extremely naive young person in a style suited to that naiveté:

> Almost the first thing he could remember was his mother standing on a stool in the kitchen, piling tins of food into the top cupboard. On the table there were more tins: pineapple, peaches, little oranges — you could tell by the pictures. He asked her:
> What are all those tins for?
> The sun was shining through the bobbly kitchen window behind her head, and though he screwed up his eyes against the dazzle he couldn't see her face properly, but he remembered her looking down at him for what seemed a long time before she said:
> Because there's a war, dear.
> What's a war? he asked. But he could never remember what she answered. (3)

Timothy's childhood sensations are sometimes like Stephen Dedalus's: he thinks of his father "The top of his head hadn't got much hair on it" (10) as Stephen registers, "His father had a hairy face"; he is frightened at boarding school; rough boys scare him. In general the feel of the early chapters is like Joyce, but less so. Here is the problem. The reason Joyce has no successful imitators is that he did the things that he did as well as they can ever be done. Imitating Joyce always means writing inferior material. Lodge recognizes this, of course, as when he writes, "Most of us have not dreamed of measuring up to that awe-inspiring genius, but have contented ourselves with reading and raiding his work for hints, models, blueprints and lessons" (WO 69). But this is inaccurate, I believe; *Out of the Shelter*, though it makes no claim to "measure up" to Joyce, requires us to measure it against him. The obvious similarities leave us no choice. And

54

the conclusion is unfavorable to Lodge.

One of the aspects of comparison is the use of language. Joyce is one of the great modernist writers, whose language is "intricately wrought, with meticulous attention to sound and cadence, as well as to imagery and diction" (LF 247). Lodge, as a writer essentially anti-modernist, or "contemporary," uses a language more denotative, more metonymic, than Joyce's. Again, there is nothing wrong with this, but it constitutes a failure to sustain a comparison which the novel overtly invites. Likewise, Stephen Dedalus's development from infancy to choice of vocation is marked by a series of intense, luminous, at times almost mystical revelations or epiphanies. Timothy Young's emergence from his shelter is, by contrast, more mundane. His sexual initiation is given us in much clearer detail and, perhaps for that reason, seems less meaningful. And his decision to continue his schooling and aim for a university is pallid compared to Stephen's call to become a priest of the eternal imagination.

The other model for this book specifically named by its author is Henry James, specifically in his use of the "international theme." Here, as well, *Out of the Shelter* looks a bit paltry. Timothy discovers that most Americans chew gum, spend money freely because they have a lot, and live for the present. Compared with the cultural contrasts in James, these are coarse, lacking in nuance.

In short, it is an oddly provocative tactic for Lodge to invite these comparisons with Joyce and James. In some ways he seems to be using this novel to enact some of the typology of his essay "The Modern, the Contemporary, and the Importance of Being Amis" from *Language of Fiction*. Joyce and James are two of his chief exhibits in this very penetrating essay, which argues that fiction in Britain is no longer "modern," but, with few exceptions, "contemporary." The contemporary differs from the modern in having a more common-sense understanding of what *life* is, and in writing about it in "ordinary prose discourse" (245). This is the same typology which Lodge returns to in his later criticism, where he distinguishes the two antithetical impulses as modernism and antimodernism, symbolism and realism, metaphor and metonymy. In any of these pairings David Lodge would range the bulk of his own writing (wistfully) in the latter group. He is primarily contemporary, while the authors he most admires, including Joyce above all, are modernist. Perhaps we should see *Out of the Shelter* as a "contemporary" homage to its author's "modern" predecessors. But if that is the aim, it seems to me unsuccesful.

One sign of the author's uneasiness, as I take it, is the use of an Epilogue to clarify the novel's themes. Now Epilogues are to be found in three of

Lodge's first four books. In *The British Museum is Falling Down* it is an integral part of the novel; it consists of Barbara's meditations following immediately after Adam's portion of the book ceases, and I suppose it *qualifies* as an epilogue only because of the shift in focus. In *Ginger, You're Barmy*, the Epilogue explains what happened to the characters after the impulsive action (discarding the contraceptives) which ended the main narrative; and in that book the Epilogue is paired with a Prologue, the two of which jointly establish a "present-time" frame for the "past-time" narrative of army life.

The Epilogue of *Out of the Shelter* seems to me unfortunate in almost every way. One of its purposes seems to be to mitigate the sudden and dramatic ending of the main narrative (Don triumphs over decadent Vince and Greg, leading Kate and Timothy away from their fireworks-*cum*-Nazi-costumes party), which must seem to the author to leave too many questions unanswered. What happens to Don and Kate? Does Timothy go on to university?

These questions receive their answers in a short scene in which the grown-up Timothy, now married with children, is reunited in the United States with Kate. He is a professor traveling in the States on a Fellowship (cf. David Lodge, 1964-65), enjoying the motel pools and the life generally. Kate is unmarried, now a naturalized U.S. citizen. In a conversation rather nakedly expository, they rehash that Heidelberg summer, revealing that Vince and Greg are probably fugitives in South America, that Kate still doesn't visit her parents, and that (in case this wasn't made clear already) Timothy believes that his trip to Heidelberg "was a turning-point for me. It brought me out of my shell, enlarged my horizons. I learned an awful lot in those few weeks" (265). Perhaps mercifully, considering this flat and *cliché*-studded phraseology, Timothy is not a literary man, but a Ph.D. in planning blight. Don has been rewarded for his virtues, as he is now a full professor at Ann Arbor.

Timothy feels a momentary fear that "happiness was only a ripening target for fate; that somewhere, around the corner, some disaster awaited him, as he blithely approached" (270), and this indicates that despite his success and happiness he has never quite lost his shelter mentality. But it seems perfunctory.

The whole Epilogue seems perfunctory, in fact, as well as leaden and damp, and nervous about leaving loose ends. The novel would probably be better without it and I am a bit surprised that the author did not omit it when he revised the book for its 1985 reissue.

What is most surprising, after all, about *Out of the Shelter* is that it is

Lodge's fourth published novel, not his first. We have his word that it was written earlier than *The British Museum is Falling Down*, though how *much* earlier is not clear. It has a number of traits traditionally associated with first novels: it is autobiographical, or at least much more so than Lodge's other books; it is written in the *Bildungsroman* form, with a single protagonist who, if not the narrator technically, is nevertheless the focal character; and it assumes that the events of that protagonist's life have greater symbolic resonance, more *gravitas*, than they actually do. It is also a tamer novel, less risk-taking, than those which immediately preceded and followed it. That is why I believe it is a step back into the shelter.

Chapter Seven

MATURITY
CHANGING PLACES

With his next novel, *Changing Places: A Tale of Two Campuses* (1975), Lodge returned to what was best in the early work, polished and perfected it, and added new strengths. That novel and the next two books — *How Far Can You Go?* and *Small World* — share several traits. One is self-conscious literary experimentation. None of these books is conventional or traditional; in each the author has invented original forms for the exploration of his material. More important, I believe, is a trait of construction. None of these books is *unitary*, in the way of *Out of the Shelter*. That novel had a single protagonist, through whom the narrative was focalized; the events of his life — his impressions, his discoveries about life, his growth — were the exclusive subject of the novel. This permitted none of the irony, the crosscutting, the strange or funny juxtapositions, the dialectical play, which animated the earlier novels. *Ginger, You're Barmy* is, as we have seen, a binary book, only a little more interested in its narrator Jon than in its title character Mike. *The Picturegoers* is a genuine ensemble work, and *The British Museum is Falling Down*, despite Adam's centrality, has an ensemble feel because of Adam's own multifariousness in the parodic fantasies.

Perhaps Lodge uses dual or multiple foci because that construction seems more enjoyable or congenial to him — he explains that "I tend to balance things against each other" (Haffenden 152). Or perhaps it is part of his reaction, increasingly evident in the seventies and eighties, against the "well-made" novel. Perhaps it is even because he is not as good at creating vivid characters as he is at handling complex arrangements of plot and counterplot, incident and motif. A novel like *Out of the Shelter* needs a more rounded, more warm-blooded, more *interesting* person at the center than Timothy Young: perhaps more interesting than David Lodge can put there. Whether this is the reason why his succeeding novels have been like *Changing Places* rather than like *Out of the Shelter*, I do not know. But the change is entirely praiseworthy. Beginning with *Changing Places*, David Lodge has earned the stature he now enjoys as one of England's best novelists.

* * * * *

In 1969 David Lodge was visiting Associate Professor at the University of California in Berkeley. That was a particularly good time to be visiting in that place, as it gave him the opportunity to witness the "Youth Revolution" very much at first hand, and he became involved peripherally in the struggles for the People's Park, a bit of waste ground which students and hippies wanted to turn into a park in opposition to the University's intention to make playing fields. Lodge has written a straightforward chronicle of the events he witnessed there in an essay called "The People's Park and the Battle of Berkeley," reprinted in *Write On*. Another essay in that collection ("The Bowling Alley and the Sun, Or, How I Learned to Stop Worrying and Love America") describes Lodge's first visit to America, in 1964-65, and his generally positive reaction to it. A light is shed on *Changing Places* by the statement that

> America is a country peculiarly rich in euphoria, and one becomes more and more conscious of this the further one drives west (a British friend and I amused ourselves in California with the creation of a mythical university on the western seaboard called Euphoric State . . .). (WO 7)

In *Changing Places* one of the two campuses to which the subtitle refers is *Euphoric State*. The reality of the place, if not the name, has changed a bit; instead of being a school where students study surfing and sun-bathing (the point of the joke in 1965), it is now a thinly disguised Berkeley, where a British academic (not a thinly disguised Lodge) has a number of enlarging experiences, some political, some sexual, and some euphoric.

Another way in which Lodge's own experience has been incorporated into *Changing Places* is that its use of academia is now an insider's view. *The British Museum is Falling Down* treats the University English Department from a distance and through the lens of the confused and baffled semi-outsider Adam Appleby. Now the author gives us a more detailed look at the operations of two very different English departments, at Euphoric State and at the other campus, Rummidge University in England.

This is a binary book with a vengeance. That is, it employs the well-chosen occasion of a transatlantic academic exchange for some witty comparison between the two cultures of England and America. Interweaving scenes of the two men's activities in their unfamiliar surroundings, Lodge emphasizes coincidences and ironic juxtapositions. Each becomes involved in political dispute, for instance: in Euphoria, Philip Swallow, the

Englishman, takes part in the battle for the People's Garden. Back in Rummidge, his American counterpart Morris Zapp is embroiled in a contretemps of much less explosive proportions, with a spate of student activism which Zapp smoothly handles being followed by a potentially violent dispute over promotions in the English Department and Zapp's informal assumption of control there.

The novel's use of twin *foci* (Swallow and Zapp) and twin *loci* (Rummidge and Euphoria) gives rise to an enormously complex system of intercut scenes, fertile with simple parallels, ironic parallels, contrasts, and other witty relationships. For instance, in the chapter called "Settling," detailing the process each undergoes of learning about his new surroundings, a scene in which Zapp wonders about BBC Radio One is followed by Swallow's introduction to a radical FM station in Plotinus; each man meets the other's wife by accident and in odd circumstances; each visits a strip-joint at exactly the same time (Lodge emphasizes that Philip Swallow goes in the afternoon, a necessary point for simultaneity given the eight-hour time difference between Esseph – the imaginary state in which Euphoria State University is located – and England).

One of the purposes of such paired scenes is satire, on both the U.S. and England. The two observers, Morris Zapp and Philip Swallow, have very different stances, and this affects the satire in a striking way. Philip Swallow is eager to go to Euphoria, having spent some blissful time in Esseph several years earlier and retaining a romantic affection for America and Americans, and the novel makes clear that this is in fact a wonderful city. Moreover, Swallow is an academic nonentity, posted to a high-powered Department of English where he remains a bit in awe. He is hardly a sharp critic of the world in which he spends his part of the exchange. Morris Zapp, very much by contrast, has never wanted to go abroad (his motto is "Travel Narrows") and has "neither affection nor respect for the British" (47); he has accepted the exchange only to get away from his wife without the embarrassment of a public estrangement; Rummidge has none of the advantages of Esseph, and the university is a perfectly ordinary metropolitan redbrick one. Obviously he has more to regret about his situation.

Add to this that his personality is very different – he is brash, arrogant, sarcastic, certain of his own superiority to his environment – and it is no surprise that Zapp makes most of the good specific satirical points. Rummidge is a dump, expensive, cold, and almost devoid of nightlife. The departmental message-board, with scrawled notes from tutors to students, is comically archaic – "as a system for conveying information it was the funniest thing he'd seen in years" (60). The strip-club he goes to in Soho is freezing and unerotic. His colleagues are, by an American's standards, unacademic — that is, they don't publish, they aren't go-getters.

Philip Swallow takes to Euphoria in a way that Morris Zapp never does to Rummidge (though Zapp briefly fantasizes about settling there and putting the department to rights). Philip never develops the kind of critique of America that Morris does of England, though it seems to me that lurking under his wonder the author has uneasy questions about the values of the America Philip Swallow swallows so eagerly: particularly the facile philosophy of liberation, ultimately a hedonistic indulgence, of the young, the craving for the new, maybe even the lack of traditions. Nevetheless, this is an unusual novel of its type, in being more balanced in its criticism of English and American ways than most and, if unbalanced, then biased towards America. David Lodge is unusually fond of America and unusually able to see the shortcomings of his own country from the perspective of an American visitor.

Changing Places is not just a dual picture of two countries and two academies as seen by each other's aliens. It has a plot, which, in Lodge's characteristic way, is full of incidents artfully arranged. At the outset Philip Swallow and Morris Zapp are both on airplanes flying to their new countries; their thoughts and reactions are continually contrasted during the flights, giving a good deal of exposition of their characters and their situations. Each meets a fellow-countryman who will prove important later on. Morris Zapp's new acquaintance is Mary Makepeace, who is flying to England for an abortion (it turns out that this charter flight is *filled*, except for Morris, with American women flying to England for abortions). She is a Roman Catholic made pregnant by a priest: this is the only Catholic element in this novel. Zapp argues against the abortion. Philip Swallow, meanwhile, has encountered Charles Boon, a former undergraduate student of his who, to his chagrin, patronizes Swallow and tells him that he, Boon, is an important figure in politics and the media in Euphoria.

Chapter Two, "Settling," continues the contrapuntal narrative of Swallow's and Zapp's acclimatization to their new locations. Swallow is quickly introduced to hippies, easy-going academic manners, and faculty gossip. Zapp, more sourly, meets almost no one except his landlord, Dr. O'Shea, and the doctor's primitive Irish niece, Bernadette. Each man meets the other's wife. Philip Swallow meets Desiree Zapp at a faculty party; Hilary Swallow comes to the faculty office and encouters Morris Zapp. Swallow goes to a party given by his young neighbors, smokes marijuana, and ends up in bed with a girl named Melanie. Each man goes to a strip show, and each is surprised by an immediate coincidence. Zapp discovers Mary Makepeace, the girl from the abortion flight, working, unaborted, as a stripper. As he emerges from the strip-club Swallow meets Melanie and through her influence Charles Boon soon becomes his room-mate.

The next chapter, "Corresponding," is epistolary, consisting of letters between the two men and their wives. These reveal that Philip's infidelity has become known to Hilary and, more, that Melanie is Morris Zapp's daughter, and that, just as Charles Boon has moved in with Philip, so Mary Makepeace has turned up again for Morris and he has installed her as lodger in the Swallow residence. The coincidences which have been a continuing feature of the plot intensify in this chapter. For instance, each man's actions are reported to his wife in an anonymous letter. Thus Bernadette writes to Mrs. Zapp about the "yaller-hared whoor" she thinks Zapp is keeping at the Swallow home. The more accurate information about Philip Swallow's adultery has been supplied by a man named Howard Ringbaum, the victim of one of Swallow's games called Humiliation. Impelled to admit that he has never read *Hamlet*, Ringbaum has been denied tenure and blames Swallow. Likewise both men's wives indicate a new awareness of Women's Liberation, marking in both cases (particularly Hilary Swallow's) a more self-reliant and aggressive posture.

Events move more headily in the next section, called "Reading" and consisting of newspaper stories. They announce the heating up of student activism on the two campuses, local and quickly cooled at Rummidge, wilder and more dangerous at Euphoria where Swallow is actually arrested. Similarly we discover that the two men have both lost their lodgings, through newspaper accounts of a mudslide which wrecked Philip's apartment and the destruction of the top floor of Dr. O'Shea's house (and thus Morris's flat) by a block of frozen urine falling from an airliner.

Various strands of the plot come to a climax in "Changing." Made homeless by the mudslide, Philip moves in with Desiree Zapp and eventually they become lovers. Meanwhile Zapp moves in with Hilary, and after a longer delay they also begin an affair. Philip Swallow becomes an unlikely campus hero, through his entirely innocent arrest, charged with stealing bricks for the People's Garden. Invited on the Charles Boon radio call-in show he fields a call which proves to be from Hilary in England and tells her of his affair on the air. Zapp more or less takes over the department at Rummidge, becoming *de facto* head of English and eventually being offered the Professorship.

Whew! The last chapter is the most original thing in this very original novel. All four Zapps and Swallows convene in New York to decide what to do with their lives. Their discussions are inconclusive and, following some academic talk between Morris and Philip on the principles of closure and the difference between novels and films, the novel simply stops. This chapter is in the form of a filmscript, and it ends with a freeze frame.

This dazzling plot seems to me designed to enable Lodge to achieve several things. One is the traditional aim of the academic novel, a comedy of manners, usually sharpened by the presence in the academy of an outsider — a foreigner (e.g. Bradbury's *Stepping Westward*), a temperamental alien (Amis's *Lucky Jim*, Howard Jacobson's *Coming From Behind*), or a non-academic only temporarily in residence (Randall Jarrell's *Pictures From an Institution*). In this case Lodge varies the usual pattern, which is to introduce one observer who is the reader's source of norms for judging the institution. By using two such observers in two different institutions, he not only achieves a "duplex chronicle" (7) but introduces a relativistic note into the satire. America judged by England is strange, but so is England judged by America.

Another purpose of the book becomes clear when we consider the wonderful ramifications of the title. Unlike *Trading Places*, which it superficially resembles, this one has shades and nuances of meaning. Obviously it means exchanging places, and that is the basic situation of the book. But it also means, I believe, places of change, places that change the people in them. The change is most visible in Philip Swallow, who spends six months in his changing place and at the end of them is healthier, physically more attractive, confident and easy-going, a man with a new wealth of experience. The Philip Swallow who went to Euphoria was a timid introvert who wished he could dance. This new man has smoked dope, taken part in a minor orgy, driven a Corvair at high speed through the hills and canyons, had affairs with two attractive women, spent time in jail. And he is fully conscious of what has come over him. He

> felt himself finally converted to expatriation; and he saw himself, too, as part of a great historical process — a reversal of that cultural Gulf Stream which had in the past swept so many Americans to Europe in search of Experience. Now it was not Europe but the West Coast of America that was the furthest rim of experiment in life and art, to which one made one's pilgrimage in search of liberation and enlightenment . . . He thought of James's *The Ambassadors* and Strether's injunction to Little Bilham, in the Paris garden, to "Live . . . live all you can; it's a mistake not to" . . . . (194-95)

Given this geography of innocence and experience, it is inevitable that Morris Zapp must change less or at least less dramatically. He undergoes no spiritual liberation, feels no enlightenment. But he has changed. The midlife crisis which had accompanied his estrangement from Desiree – a suspicion of his own irrelevance, doubts about his abilities in the classroom, loss of sexual appeal – has been assuaged by the months in Rummidge. His almost effortless dominance of the academic life of the university has restored his confidence, and along with it he has become accustomed to the more old-fashioned rhythms of life in England, even "getting used to the quaint meterological idiom" of imprecise weather forecasting. "He accepted that, like so much British usage, it was a language of evasion and compromise, designed to take the drama out of the weather" (200). Before long, happy with Hilary, he is actually considering settling in Rummidge. After his acid beginnings there, it is a remarkable change.

Perhaps most telling, in the multiple meanings of *Changing Places*, is its indication that Morris Zapp and Philip Swallow have changed the places, changed Rummidge and Euphoria. Philip has, from what we can tell, had little adademic effect on his host institution, though he is indirectly responsible for the dismissal of Howard Ringbaum and the retention in his surprisingly vacated place of Karl Kroop, a controversial lecturer originally slated to be fired. Since Keep Kroop was one of the rallying cries of the student activists, Philip has contributed to their cause here as well as, equally inadvertently, in the People's Garden.

Morris Zapp makes a bigger splash at Rummidge. For instance, by persuading Mary Makepeace to have her baby and later arranging for her to lodge with Hilary Swallow, he has introduced Hilary to a knowledge of Women's Liberation which will change the terms of her marriage to Philip. Likewise he is involved in the resignation of Gordon Masters, Head of English, and as his virtual replacement makes the crucial recommendation that Philip Swallow be promoted to Senior Lecturer over a probably more qualified colleague. As we shall see in *Small World* and *Nice Work*, Philip Swallow's career takes wing from this beginning, and he becomes Head of the Department and later Dean of the Faculty of Arts.

All these purposes of the "duplex" plot are suggested by the narrator's remark on the second page of the book. Having called attention to the fact that the two men are in airplanes approaching each other over the North Pole – urging the similarity of their fates and the possible conjunction of them – he goes on to suggest that it would not be surprising . . . if two men changing places for six months should exert a reciprocal influence on each other's destinies, and actually mirror each other's experience in certain respects, notwithstanding all the differences that exist between the two environments, and between the characters of the two men and their respective attitudes towards the whole enterprise. (8)

Well, yes, it wouldn't be surprising if there were some mirroring incidents, some reciprocal experiences, even between two men so different as Morris Zapp and Philip Swallow and two places so markedly unlike as Rummidge and Euphoria. But Lodge has zestfully gone over the top into wholly unlikely, and therefore deliciously artificial, similarities and coincidences. I have mentioned some of them — for instance, the coincidence that, at the same time, the two men's wives receive anonymous letters accusing the husbands of sexual misconduct; that they attend strip-shows, both for the first time, at exactly the same time; that Zapp makes love to Swallow's wife, while Swallow has affairs first with Zapp's daughter and then with his wife. I have not mentioned the presence, in Philip Swallow's lavatory, of a volume containing a Morris Zapp essay, a vicious anonymous review of which appeared years earlier in the *TLS*: a discovery which persuades Zapp for a time that Swallow is his enemy. At the beginning of the book the narrator elaborates on the symmetry of the two planes containing the two professors almost meeting over the Pole, but passing "unremarked by anyone other than the narrator of this duplex chronicle" (7). It should be no surprise, then, that the jets bringing Morris and Hilary from England and Philip and Desiree from Esseph to New York do more than pass; they almost collide in mid-air.

What is the purpose of this elaborate pattern of inter-connection? I think there are two aims involved. One is this. Having decided on a "duplex chronicle" in which the narrative will explore the similar experiences of two dissimilar men on an academic exchange, Lodge has chosen to explore to the limit: to push the symmetry as far as it can possibly go.

The other is more important. The effect of these very far-fetched coincidences is to call attention to the artifice of the novel. Mere coincidence *need not* violate the realistic illusion, or rather need not notify us that the novelist wishes to violate that illusion. In *Ginger, You're Barmy* we may decide, on reflection, that the odds against Mike Brady's IRA unit raiding the depot in which Jon Browne is standing guard on his last night in the army are almost prohibitively long. But that sort of coincidence is unremarkable in fiction; it is not only part of the novelist's permitted economy of means, but one of the ways in which he makes art more *meaningful* than real life. Very likely it is only on reflection, or when we are dissatisfied with the novel for other reasons, that we find objections. In novels really riddled with coincidence, like those of Dickens or Hardy, we understand that they exist to demonstrate the ways of either Providence or a malign Fate.

But Lodge is doing something else; he not only devises extraodinary coincidences for Swallow and Zapp, he calls attention to them. As Morris Zapp looks into the strip-tease establishments of London, he thinks of the ones in Esseph, "Which at this very moment Philip Swallow is now observing for the first time" (111); Morris thinks

> "Why not?' and ducks into the very next strip-joint he comes to, under the nose of a disconsolate-looking Indian at the door. And "Why not?" thought Philip Swallow. (112)

There are a great many such juxtapositions in the novel, all designed to bring out as fully as possible the author's role in arranging things this way. Instead of hiding his artifices, Lodge flaunts them. Instead of trying to "disguise the fact that a novel is discontinuous with real life" (LF 42), this one celebrates that discontinuity.

This is because *Changing Places* is a metafictional, or self-conscious, novel. In it Lodge has turned his back on the realistic principle that novels should imitate real life as closely and unobtrusively as possible so that the reader of an ideally successful novel would be unaware of the difference between the book and the real life it proposed to imitate. The self-conscious novel sets out to make any such confusion impossible and the idea of it funny. Robert Alter defines the "fully-selfconscious novel" as

> one in which from beginning to end, through the style, the handling of narrative viewpoint, the names and words imposed on the characters, the patterning of the narration, the nature of the characters and what befalls them, there is a consistent effort to convey to us a sense of the fictional world as an authorial construct set up against a background of literary tradition and convention. (xi)

The main devices Lodge uses in this novel for flaunting its fictionality are the obtrusion of the narrative presence, the use of a built-in commentary on the novel, and the complexity of form. The first of these is, of course, a trait this novel shares with the eighteenth and nineteenth century masters of the form like Fielding and Sterne, Trollope and Dickens. Remarks like "the crossing of their paths at the still point of the turning world passed unremarked by anyone other than the narrator of this duplex chronicle" (7), followed shortly by a digression on "the differences we can take in at a glance from our privileged narrative perspective (higher than that of any jet)" (8) are in the tradition, as are Lodge's confident use of inside views (so-called omniscience) and shifting perspectives. All these call attention to the presence of the author.

So do joke-criticisms built into the novel. One of these is the remark given to Desiree in the final chapter; commenting on the near-collision of their airplanes approaching New York, she says "It would have solved a lot of problems, of course. A spectacular finale to our little drama" (240). It is a novelist's solution, of course, and one which Lodge plays with by making the planes nearly collide.

A more sustained commentary on the novel comes from a book called *Let's Write a Novel*. This is an old manual (written in 1927 by A. J. Beamish, author of *A Fair But Frozen Maid*, *Wild Mystery*, and *Glynis of the Glen*) belonging to Philip Swallow, for which he writes in desperation when he learns that he is to teach a fiction-writing course at Euphoric. Hilary finds it too late, it is half-destroyed in the mail, and its sole function is to issue little criticisms of the novel *Changing Places*: to suggest that by traditional lights, this is *not* the way to write a novel. For instance Hilary writes to Philip, in the chapter called "Corresponding" and composed entirely of letters,

> Do you still want me to send on *Let's Write a Novel*? What a funny little book it is. There's a whole chapter on how to write an epistolary novel, but surely nobody's done that since the eighteenth century?
>
> Love from all of us here,
Hilary (130)

At the end of a long flashback which circles back from Philip Swallow's arrival at his office to fill in the history of his affair with Desiree Zapp, he opens a package, discovers *Let's Write a Novel*, and reads at random: "Flashbacks should be used sparingly, if at all. They slow down the progress of the story and confuse the reader. Life, after all, goes forwards, not backwards" (186). And Morris Zapp has also read out a short passage which insists that "The best kind of story is the one with a happy ending; the next best is the one with an unhappy ending, and the worst kind is the story that has no ending at all" (88). This is of course the kind of story in *Changing Places*.

The final means by which this novel flaunts its artificiality is in its heterogeneity of format. It has six chapters. Three of them contain the intertwined narratives of Swallow and Zapp, narrated in a fairly conventional even if "duplex" way. The other three call rather more attention to themselves. One of them, for instance, is composed entirely of letters. Another is all newspaper clippings. Though such impersonal media might seem to deny the author's responsibility for the contents (this is after all one of the proudest claims of the originators, like Richardson) the effect is, instead, to call attention to the technique and thus the technician. Lodge calls this a "Joycean variety of styles," alluding to the different techniques of the episodes in *Ulysses*, and gives two reasons for it: a desire "to keep the reader guessing and on his toes" seems overly modest; more in keeping with what I have been discussing as the self-consciousness of this work is his explanation of

the English way with self-conscious artifice in the novel: breaking the frame of realistic illusion, disturbing the smooth surface of a homogenous prose style with abrupt shifts of tone and register, are licensed as *comic* strategies. (WO 68)

The last chapter in the novel is the most striking. It is not narrative at all but a film-script. Like letters or clippings, the script poses as objective, autonomous. Lodge shows that it is as manipulative as narrative. It also permits, as narrative cannot, a *suspension* of the novel, a much more complete refusal to come to an ending than J. Walter Beamish could ever imagine. The chapter turns to discussion between Swallow and Zapp about the difference between fiction and film, Swallow insisting on their discontinuity, Zapp asserting their similarity "at the structural level." Swallow brings the book to a close with this bravura passage:

PHILIP. That's it. Well, that's something the novelist can't help giving away, isn't it, that his book is shortly coming to an end? It may not be a happy ending, nowadays, but he can't disguise the tell-tale compression of the pages. . . . I mean, mentally you brace yourself for the ending of a novel. As you're reading, you're aware of the fact that there's only a page or two left in the book, and you get ready to close it. But with a film there's no way of telling, especially nowadays, when films are much more loosely structured, much more ambivalent, than they used to be. There's no way of telling which frame is going to be the last. The film is going along, just as life goes along, people are behaving, doing things, drinking, talking, and we're watching them, and at any point the director chooses, without warning, without anything being resolved, or explained, or wound up, it can just . . . end.

PHILIP shrugs. The camera stops, freezing him in mid-gesture.

THE END (251)

Chapter Eight

CATHOLICS IN THE WORLD
HOW FAR CAN YOU GO?

The next novel, published in 1980, is as much a step forward in one way as *Changing Places* was in another. Lodge gets to grips with the serious issues involved in being Catholic in England more fully than in any previous work. As part of this effort, perhaps, academic concerns move to the periphery. That is not to say that any of Lodge's novels is unconcerned with university education. In this one, all the Roman Catholic characters meet at University College, London, two of them become dons and another marries one, and there is much taking of courses among the others. Though this may sound like a novel suffused with academia, the academic life is part of the background, part of the normal flow of events for serious and educated young people in the sixties and seventies.

But it may also be misleading to say that this novel is about Catholicism. Though Lodge himself identifies its subject as "the practical effects of Vatican II on Catholic liturgy, devotional practice and general life-styles, both clerical and lay" (WO 36), it is about more than that: about the very large question of the beliefs by which men and women live; about the changes which human lives undergo as time passes; about the frustration of hopes, the ironic fulfillment of wishes, and the consolations available for disappointment and failure. It is in almost every way David Lodge's most ambitious novel. It has a breadth of scope that all his earlier novels lack.

One result (or cause?) of this breadth is that he is working, once again, with a large cast of characters. As I have pointed out, Lodge's novels usually fall into one of two types. One type is unitary—by which I mean with a single focal character—like *Out of The Shelter* and, despite stylistic exfoliation, *The British Museum Is Falling Down*. The other is dual or binary, like *Ginger, You're Barmy, Changing Places*, or *Nice Work*. This mode seems particularly congenial to the author, more so than the unitary, which in *Out of the Shelter* produced some problematic results. Once before, indeed, in *The Picturegoers*, he organized a large number of characters in an ensemble work. In *How Far Can You Go?* he does it again. In both books the nature of Catholicism was in question and particularly the relationship (usually a conflict) between the spiritual and secular life; in both books the characters display a range of possible attitudes; both books show a highly patterned artfulness of form, manipulating the many characters and their separate stories in a complex dance-like movement.

Three possible qualities which this sort of book naturally possesses are (1) difficulty in following the plots; (2) thinness of characterization because there are too many characters; and (3) an important, even magisterial, authorial or narratorial presence holding the strands together. I say that they are *natural* qualities of this novel, but not inevitable ones. Both *The Picturegoers* and *How Far Can You Go?* successfully avoid the threat of confusion posed by the multiple plots and centers of interest. This is a result of good planning on the author's part as well as careful management of the plot lines and careful though unobtrusive transitions between them. In *The Picturegoers* the author's art conceals art, and it is only on reflection that we comprehend how nicely it has all been arranged. In *How Far Can You Go?* (as I will explain more fully later on), the author has reasons for declaring his artfulness, and we are invited to watch how he does it. In the first chapter, having introduced ten major characters, all taking part in an early weekday Mass, he invites us to

> remind yourselves who they are. Ten characters is a lot to take in all at once, and soon there will be more, because we are going to follow their fortunes, in a manner of speaking, up to the present, and obviously they are not going to pair off with each other, that would be too neat, too implausible, so there will be other characters not yet invented, husbands and wives and lovers, not to mention parents and children, so it is important to get these ten straight now. Each character, for instance, has already been associated with some selected detail of dress or appearance which should help you to distinguish one from another. Such details also carry connotations which symbolize certain qualities or attributes of the character. Thus Angela's very name connotes angel . . . and her blonde hair archetypecasts her as the fair virtuous woman . . . (14)

This flaunting of the mechanisms of the novel is part of its metafictional play; but of course this introduction does help the reader in sorting out the characters, their traits and their lives, and is no less useful for this public reminder of why it is given to us.

Another possible consequence of the multiplex novel is thinness of characterization. I have suggested that the creation of richly alive characters is not David Lodge's strength at any time. In *The Picturegoers* most of the people do suffer from two-dimensionality and some are close to being cliches. The most fully fleshed is Mark Underwood.

In *How Far* twenty years of novelistic practice bear fruit in a more real-seeming cast. Again, there are exceptions, but of course every novel has its minor characters whom the author, perhaps just as a matter of economy, has not given a rounded form, and in this is it like our own lives, populated by countless people, all but a few of whom are "unrealistic" or "flat," credible and interesting to us only as they participate in the plots of our lives. The advance in *How Far* is in the number of persons to whom Lodge has imparted the kind of life which we find in the best fictional characters. Some of the ten introduced in Chapter One never become major — Miles, the public school boy and repressed homosexual, never amounts to much — and others, though often present, sound much the same note throughout the twenty five years covered here. But seven or eight of them, to whom we may add two or three wives, are convincingly there as characters, capable of changing credibly and surprising us convincingly. A novelist is always forced to choose how he will marshal his resources, knowing that greater breadth must be purchased by loss of depth. Considering the great breadth of this book, its ambitious chronicling of twenty-five years of change in the lives of some dozen adults, played out against the background (also chronicled) of radical change in British society and in the Roman Catholic Church, Lodge achieves remarkable depth in the people.

The final quality, hardly a fault, to which the broad ensemble work is subject is an important authorial or narratorial presence at the center of the discourse. *The Picturegoers* and *How Far Can You Go?* both possess this quality, though in radically different form.

The Picturegoers is largely composed of many "objective" views, both external and internal (transcriptions of thoughts), of a whole series of characters loosely connected by attendance at the cinema or church. The narrator does not overtly call attention to himself in the usual ways — refer to himself in the first person, express opinions, comment on his own perspicuity, generalize on the action — but an alert reading must make us aware of the strong, central authorial or narratorial presence all the same. Wayne Booth long ago dispelled the misconception that discourse of the kind we find, say, in Joyce's novels is "objective," that there the author is "absent." What Stephen Dedalus says about the removal of the author above or behind his own creation may be an ideal for modern fiction, but it is one which Joyce and those who write in his tradition fail to realize. The book in which the stream of consciousness of one character is given to us in rich detail (e.g. *A Portrait of the Artist as a Young Man*, or in Lodge's work, *Out of the Shelter*) raises the question, "who knows all this about the contents of a boy's mind? Who tells us this?" And these questions call far *more* insistently for answer in a work like *Ulysses*, which delivers inside views of many characters. There, we ask as well, "who is the arranger?" Despite the supposed ideal of "objectivity," there can be few readers of *Ulysses* who have not been aware of the author during their reading. *The Picturegoers* has this same sort of authorial presence — implicit but insistent. We are aware of a privileged observer and artful arranger.

In *How Far Can You Go?* the narrator is much more visible. No longer silently powerful, he is here more like what Malcolm Bradbury has called "the novelist as impresario." In *Possibilities*, his book on the state of the novel dedicated to David Lodge, Bradbury explains what he takes to be behind the problematic appearances of the novelist in *The French Lieutenant's Woman*:

> If it is the case that we live in a time when it is difficult for a writer to establish the literal reality of plot and character as coherent meanings, and to express a fiction as a coherent linear development of knowledge; if language and structure have become quizzical properties for many of our writers, then Fowles is clearly an author who has come to know and explore such suspicions. (262)

How Far Can You Go? is a novel very much concerned with the evanescence of meaning and convention — both in religion and in art — and this concern is displayed in the role of the narrator. His management of the novel is foregrounded in various ways. One of them is the quite traditional transitional remark — like "Before we go any further it would probably be a good idea to explain the metaphysic or world-picture these young people had acquired from their Catholic upbringing and education" (6). This will be familiar to anyone who has read Dickens or George Eliot. The shifts from one plot to a related one or from narration to exposition or the reverse ("But enough of this philophisizing" [121]) are part of the omniscient narrator's omnipresence or multifariousness, his superiority in perspective to the limits of the material he relates. In *Changing Places* the narrator refers to the same phenomenon when he discerns, between Philip Swallow and Morris Zapp (both flying in airplanes at the time) "differences we can take in at a glance from our privileged narrative altitude (higher than that of any jet)" (8).

The omnipresence is temporal as well as spatial; instead of being linked to the "present" of the story, the narrator freely relates future events,

73

usually as ironic commentary on the "present," as when an account of Michael and Miriam's honeymoon in 1958 parts to reveal Michael's memory of it in 1968 and an account of it given in 1975 before snapping back to the story's "present" of 1958. There are a number of such "future" commentaries on the "present" in this book, most of which serve either to demonstrate how much the world, and the characters in this book, will change even though they cannot "now" imagine it. Again, this kind of freedom is part of the conventional technique of the omniscient novelist.

A bit more surprising are bits of the narrator's discourse which call attention to the fictiveness of the story: "Tessa, in short, was classically ripe for having an affair, and in another milieu, or novel, might well have had one" (154). Or, "The omniscience of novelists has its limits, and we shall not attempt to trace here the process of cogitation, debate, intrigue, fear, anxious prayer and unconscious motivation which finally produced" the Papal decision on birth control, *Humanae Vitae* (114). These are the kinds of narrator's discourse which, we are sometimes told, "break the illusion" of reality to which the novel traditionally is presumed to aspire. In this novel David Lodge goes out of his way to make the illusion of reality impossible; we cannot think of characters as real people when the narrator himself *calls* them "characters," when we see him in the act of making them up and assigning them names, when he reminds us that they are just "fictional characters" who "cannot bleed or weep" (125).

The narrator reminds us from time to time not just that he is a novelist, but that he is David Lodge. He tells us about Dennis's National Service experience in a few words, then reminds us that "I have described it in detail elsewhere" (37) — in other words, in *Ginger, You're Barmy*. His first critical book seems to be slyly meant when "Tessa offered to lend Roy a book on the language of fiction that she had found particularly useful" (181). The last section of the novel is in the form of a transcript of a television documentary program which records the Paschal Festival of Catholics for an Open Church and includes all the characters we have been following in their twenty-five years of change. In the transcript all the speakers (in voice-over) are identified except one; we know, though, that that voice belongs to the author, who has, like John Fowles in *The French Lieutenant's Woman*, put the author into the frame of the fiction. One paragraph summarizes the lives of the characters after the Paschal Festival and the storm which its televising provoked and ends with "I teach English literature at a redbrick university and write novels in my spare time, slowly, and hustled by history" (243). Lodge's comment on the same sort of irruption in a novel by Kurt Vonnegut is

This not only displays the author's hand in his work; it throws the reader completely off balance by bringing the real, historic author on to the same plane as his own fictitious characters and at the very same time drawing attention to their fictitiousness. (WWS 15).

An even more flamboyant example of authorial irruption is in Chapter Three where the narrator comments on the Rhythm Method of family planning, explains "I have written about this before," summarizes the plot of *The British Museum Is Falling Down*, comments on its critical reception and how he now thinks of the book, and even quotes a fan letter about it which he received from a Czech reader.

What is the purpose of all this? What, even more oddly, is the purpose of illuminating the narrative with commentary from literary theory? The best example of *this* practice is the narrator's invocation of Gérard Genette to comment on the decorum of representing married sex in fiction.

Once or twice a week, perhaps, if they happened to go to bed at the same time, and Angela was not feeling too tired, they made love. It is difficult to do justice to ordinary married sex in a novel. There are too many acts for them all to be described, and usually no particular reason to describe one act rather than another; so the novelist falls back on summary, which sounds dismissive. As a contemporary French critic has pointed out in a treatise on narrative, a novelist can (a) narrate once what happened once or (b) narrate *n* times what happened once or (c) narrate *n* times what happened *n* times or (d) narrate once what happened *n* times. Seductions, rapes, the taking of new lovers or the breaking of old taboos, are usually narrated according to (a), (b) or (c). Married love in fiction tends to be narrated according to mode (d). (150)

What is the purpose? Well, to some exent it is the purpose of all self-conscious fiction written under the special problematic conditions described above by Malcolm Bradbury. Lodge himself has often written on this subject; it is a particular focus of his criticism, and this novel, which incorporates literary criticism and theory into its discourse, exemplifies some of his ideas about the situation of the novel. He describes how the postmodernist novel tries to frustrate interpretation,

administer a shock to the reader and thus resist assimilation into conventional categories of the literary. Ways of doing this include:

combining in one work the apparently factual and the obviously fictional, introducing the author and the question of authorship into the text, and exposing conventions in the act of using them. (WWS 15)

The description of the "problematic novel" Lodge writes in *The Novelist at the Crossroads* (24 ff.) is similar. Thus the post-modernist devices comment on the impossibility of the traditional relationships between reader and narrative and between narrative and "real life."

Typically, though, David Lodge is not committed to the complete abolition of traditional literary responses. The best evidence of his lingering realism is in the presentation of the death of Angela and Dennis's child. The narration of this event is curiously off-hand and immediately qualified by a narratorial comment preventing naive illusion:

Two years after Nicole [their child with Downs' syndrome] was born, Dennis and Angela's next youngest child, Anne, was knocked down by a van outside their house and died in hospital a few hours later. I have avoided a direct presentation of this incident because frankly I find it too painful to contemplate. Of course, Dennis and Angela and Anne are fictional characters, they cannot bleed or weep, but they stand here for all the real people to whom such disasters happen with no apparent reason or justice. One does not kill off characters lightly, I assure you, even ones like Anne, evoked solely for that purpose. (125)

This comment ought to anesthetize feeling, to establish aesthetic distance so that it would be impossible to "feel sorry" for Anne or her parents. And yet, the explanation of Anne's death, and particularly its effect on the handicapped sister Nicole, is extremely affecting: "'Where Anne?' Nicole would say for years afterwards, turning up at their bedside in the middle of the night, tugging gently on Dennis's pyjama sleeve, 'Where Anne?'" (148). That it is so demonstrates, by a circuitous route, the realist proposition that there is an essential relationship between "characters" in books and people in real life; though we need not make the naive mistake of thinking that fictional people *are* real, they stand in a symbolic relationship to the real, they stand for them. Martin Steinmann explains that "fiction of whatever kind is incorrigibly and inevitably synecdochic: its fictive particulars symbolize the wholes of which they are imaginary parts or the classes of which they are imaginary members" (303). Lodge makes the same point, and does so in a particularly striking way by insisting all the while on the fictiveness of the particulars.

There is one further point to be made about the post-modernist tutorial on reality and belief which *How Far Can You Go?* embodies. That is that the novel itself is centrally about belief and its consequences — in this case, belief in the Catholic faith. Thus the form of the book, its auto-questionings and self-underminings, accompany a chronicle of dwindling faith, growing inability to believe, and insistent challenges to the conventions, in the Church.

To begin with, there is the title of the book. *How Far Can You Go?* is, like *Changing Places* and *Small World*, a multi-dimensional title. Initially it refers to the question of sex, narrowly considered, within a Catholic framework — *"Please, Father, how far can you go with a girl, Father?"* (4) And this is a very important strain in the lives of all these Catholic young people — strain in every way: their concern for the limits of approved sex, approved either by the Church or by the girl in question, dominates several lives. As we read, the title takes on more meaning, coming to refer to how far the church can go in certain directions, mostly "liberal"; how far can it go in allowing married couples to plan their families, how far can it go in permitting nuns to behave like women in the world, how far can it approve of liberation theology, priestly challenge to dogma, and so on. The answer in most cases proves to be not far enough; and then the question becomes "How far can you go and still be a Catholic?" Of the original ten characters ranged at the communion rail, one becomes a Jehovah's Witness and then a Sufist, one returns to the Anglican Church, one spends twenty years in secular separation from the Church; others are divorced, Dennis loses his faith when Anne dies. All the married couples practice birth control, eventually, thus severing themselves from the church's teaching. Two priests leave the priesthood to marry. How far can you go?

This is an important theme, and Lodge handles it with particular success. This is the first novel, I believe, in which he has actually made being a Catholic a serious, world-historical kind of situation. Hitherto Catholicism has largely been something that interfered with sexual pleasure or at least with contraception. And it is that, still, in *How Far Can You Go?* but it is much much more. Here the author comes to grips with faith, what Catholics believe, how those beliefs change and how those changes produce ripples of change in the arena of behavior. Catholicism is much more than a source of serio-comic frustration. It is, for good or ill, the most important thing in life for most of these people. One expository passage connects the question of contraception to other, larger matters of

77

Church doctrine:

> The crisis in the Church over birth control was not, therefore, the
> absurd diversion from more important matters that it first appeared
> to many observers, for it compelled thoughtful Catholics to re-ex-
> amine and redefine their views on fundamental issues: the relation-
> ship betweeen authority and conscience, between the religious and
> lay vocations, between flesh and spirit. (120)

This is a large claim, but here the author makes it good; this novel becomes
a serious examination, through the lives of fictional characters, of exactly
these issues.

In pointing out that it is serious I mean two things. The first, and most
striking perhaps, is that this novel really is not a comedy, thus differentiat-
ing it fairly sharply from the books which immediately precede and follow
it. It has its funny moments, but the prevailing tone is more quizzical or
sorrowful than facetious. The other kind of seriousness is exactly this
grappling with important issues in a serious way, and the one which is most
novel, for David Lodge, is death. As his authorial "philosophizing" points
out, "Death, after all, is the overwhelming question to which sex provides
no answer, only an occasional brief respite from thinking about it" (121).
In David Lodge's early novels death plays no important role. There is the
bombing of Jill and her mother at the beginning of *Out of the Shelter*,
followed by the later off-stage death of her father the airman. And that is
it. Most of the novels, of course, deal with the young, so that the sad causes
of death among the old hardly come into play. In *How Far Can You Go?*
by contrast death is at hand. There is the harrowing death of Anne, the
child of Angela and Dennis, by vehicle. Angela's father dies horribly of
lung cancer. Michael has a bowel cancer scare. Add to these the long-term
schizophrenia of one of the main characters, the painful adjustment to
homosexuality of another, the marital scars of several adulteries; the book
is touched with human suffering and mortality. To list the sorrows is to
suggest melodrama, and it is not that at all: more like the statistically
probable fate of a group of ten people who were born in 1935. Again, the
novelist asks how far can you go? And in presenting the pain of real life
the answer is quite far, given his sureness of touch and tact. Again, the
reminders that the bad things happen to fictional characters, or really don't
happen at all, does little to lessen the frequent sadness of the narrative.

In addition to the depth, breadth, and maturity of Lodge's treatment
here of both Roman Catholic issues and what can only be called the issues

of human life, there is one further important point, and that is the nice dovetailing, by means of the question How far can you go? of the Catholic and literary themes. This parallel appears most explicitly in a couple of narrative comments. Having detailed the crises of faith of several of his characters, he comments:

> So they stood upon the shores of Faith and felt the old dogmas and certainties ebbing away rapidly under their feet and between their toes, sapping the foundations upon which they stood, a sensation both agreeably stimulating and slightly unnerving. For we all like to believe, do we not, if only in stories? People who find religious belief absurd are often upset if a novelist breaks the illusion of reality he has created. . . . in matters of belief (as of literary convention) it is a nice question how far you can go in this process without throwing out something vital. (142-43)

The book raises that question about Catholicism and literary convention. By showing how a cast of representative Roman Catholics steadily jettison almost everything which in 1952 defined them as Catholics, he forces the reader to decide what is essential; meanwhile the method asks the same question about fiction. The novel simultaneously examines the outer limits of religion (in the story) and fiction (in the discourse).

There is one final authoritative commentary on this subject, this one provided by the unnamed voice in the televised Paschal Festival, a voice which clearly belongs to Lodge:

> Christian belief will be different from what it used to be, what it used to be for Catholics, anyway. We must not only believe, but know that we believe, live our belief and yet see it from outside, aware that in another time, another place, we would have believed something different (indeed, did ourselves believe differently at different times and places in our lives), without feeling that this invalidates belief. Just as when reading a novel, or writing one for that matter, we maintain a double consciousness of the characters as both, as it were, real and fictitious, free and determined, and know that however absorbing and convincing we may find it, it is not the only story we shall want to read (or, as the case may be, write) but part of an endless sequence of stories by which man has sought and will always seek to make sense of life. And death. (239-40)

This statement is the real conclusion of the book. The last few pages go on to the anticlimactic or ironic consequences of the Paschal Festival and a semi-jokey farewell to the reader. In its serious, even philosophical, connection between the subject of Catholicism and the metafictional treatment of the text, no less than in its broad recognition of the ultimate questions of life and death, it makes a fitting summing up for Lodge's deepest novel.

Chapter Nine

DONS IN SPACE
SMALL WORLD

David Lodge's seventh novel represents a new direction in several ways. *Small World* was the first of his books to be shortlisted for the Booker Prize. It sold well, both in England, where it was a bestseller, and in America; there, according to Lodge, it was "a kind of breakthrough" (Marecki 303). It was made into a television series, broadcast on the Independent Television Network in Britain. In many ways it can be seen as an advance into higher visibility, wider readership, and greater critical respect.

And, after his comprehensive treatment of Catholicism and its discontents in *How Far Can You Go?*, in this book Lodge writes what is arguably the ultimate academic novel. We have seen the progression, in protagonists, from tentative graduate student (*The British Museum Is Falling Down*) to modest lecturer exchanging with academic superstar (*Changing Places*). As that novel was bi-national, exchanging an Englishman and an American, each of whom then attended to local interests, now the focus is multinational, the cast of characters is large and polyglot. Morris Zapp and Philip Swallow return, and though they are no longer the main characters, the changes they have undergone in the ten years supposed to have elapsed since they changed places provide a measure of change in academia. Morris Zapp is now an even bigger academic star than in 1969; he is no longer a Jane Austen man (*the* Jane Austen man, he would have said then), but a literary theorist of post-structuralist bent. Still at Euphoric State, he now aspires to be the highest-paid English professor in the world, while suspecting that he already may be. He and Desiree are now divorced, and she has written a best-selling feminist novel about their marriage. He no longer believes that "Travel narrows": now he travels all the time, mostly to international conferences, where he delivers the same paper again and again.

Philip Swallow has also moved up. Through chance and inadvertence, rather than solid merit, he has not only gotten the senior lectureship we saw looming at the end of *Changing Places*, but is now Head of Department at Rummidge. He and Hilary are still married, though not very happily. He now travels a good deal, too, though on a more modest scale than Zapp's; he takes British Council lecture trips to foreign lands where he

81

speaks on topics like Hazlitt to the natives and seeks adventures to alleviate his ennui. Swallow has also published a book, called *Hazlitt and the Common Reader* — as old-fashioned a book as can be imagined in the scholarly world of the late seventies, defiantly anti-theoretical, rejoicing to concur with the common reader — which has had no scholarly impact at all, has never even been reviewed.

One other sharp change which we note in *Small World* is contained in its subtitle: *An Academic Romance*. We know, then, that we are to approach this book with different expectations, and we are further reminded when among the epigraphs we find the famous disclaimer from Nathaniel Hawthorne's preface to *The House of the Seven Gables*:

> When a writer calls his work a Romance, it need hardly be observed that he wishes to claim a certain latitude, both as to its fashion and material, which he would not have felt himself entitled to assume had he professed to be writing a Novel.

This is part of Lodge's purpose in writing a romance: to claim for himself a certain latitude, a certain freedom from the "requirements" of the novel — that is, in what Hawthorne calls the "fashion" of the book. The other aim is to appropriate elements of plot already at hand (Hawthorne's "material"), along with certain structural principles which conventionally order the romantic plot. Put another way, the use of the romance both liberates and confines the author; both frees him from the requirements of verisimilitude, economy, and plausibility, and imposes structures — what Wayne Booth calls "the grooves of genre."

First, the liberation. In the Preface from which Lodge chooses his epigraph, Hawthorne goes on to explain that the novel "is presumed to aim at a very minute fidelity, not merely to the possible, but to the probable and ordinary course of man's experience." The Romancer, by contrast, need not adhere to the probable.

> He will be wise, no doubt, to make a very moderate use of the privileges here stated, and, especially, to mingle the Marvellous rather as a slight, delicate, and evanescent flavour, rather than as any portion of the actual substance of the dish offered to the public. He can hardly be said, however, to commit a literary crime, even if he disregard this caution. (xi)

Northrup Frye explains that

the hero of romance moves in a world in which the ordinary laws of nature are slightly suspended: prodigies of courage and endurance, unnatural to us, are natural to him, and enchanted weapons, talking animals, terrifying ogres and witches, and talismans of miraculous power violate no rule of probability once the postulates of romance have been established. (33)

To what extent does Lodge make use of his permission to introduce the Marvelous, his license to use talking animals and witches? Not very much, really. There is nothing in the book which is literally impossible. Instead, what is liberated in this book is an extravagant profusion of coincidences. Even this is by no means revolutionary, for Lodge; *The British Museum is Falling Down* had more than its share of coincidences, while *Changing Places* was, we might say, fundamentally structured on them. It was no coincidence that Morris Zapp and Philip Swallow changed places; but after that, it was highly coincidental that they swapped wives, that each became involved in campus political disputes, that Swallow had an affair with Zapp's daughter, that Hilary Swallow phoned Philip just while he was on a live phone-in radio show, that their airplanes almost collided over New York at the end of the novel, and so on and on. There the use of coincidence reminds us, again and again, of the fictiveness of the story and of the powers of the novelist who arranges the coincidences.

In *Small World* the coincidences have a different effect. They do, of course, remind us of the authorial mind behind the plot; but they also have a more important structural role to play. This is a novel with a very large cast of characters and an extraordinary amount of detail about the world of international academia, writing, publishing, and reviewing. The only way to make it a manageable world as well as a small one is to interrelate characters and details by what we might call over-determination.

To take just one example, one of the less important characters, but a node of several plot lines, is called Ronald Frobisher; he is a novelist, now unable to write another novel. On an airplane headed for a European conference are Howard Ringbaum (familiar from *Changing Places*) and his wife Thelma. Thelma is reading Frobisher's novel, *Could Try Harder*. Thousands of miles away Japanese academic Akira Sakazaki is translating the same book. Thelma will meet, and try to seduce, Frobisher at an awards ceremony, where Frobisher will also meet Persse McGarrigle, the central figure in the romance plot. Frobisher will attend a conference at Heidelberg, where he will meet and sleep with Desiree Zapp, Morris's ex-wife and another blocked novelist; Persse will meet Akira Sakazaki on his travels; at the MLA conference in New York Persse will ask a question which will, as a sort of side-effect, renew Desiree's and Frobisher's writing abilities. At one point Frobisher is interviewed over the radio by an Australian academic named Rodney Wainwright. Wainwright is joined to Philip Swallow in two ways; first, he has an affair with an undergraduate who transferred from Rummidge after an affair with Swallow; second, at an international conference where he is scheduled to deliver a paper (invited by Morris Zapp), he is at the point where he must soon reveal that he has not finished writing the paper, and has no real idea about the future of literary criticism, when he is interrupted by the frightening collapse of Philip Swallow. Since Swallow appears to have Legionnaire's disease, this ends the conference, clears the hotel, and converts Rodney Wainwright to pious Christianity.

We see, then, what the title means. As part of a series of pithy, multivalent titles also including *Changing Places* and *Nice Work*, it says a great deal. "It's a small world" — that is what people say in recognition of coincidence. It is an appropriate comment throughout this book, as the same people appear at every turn, reviewing each other's books, commenting on each other's papers, and interfering with each other's aspirations for love and power.

And the academic world is a small one, in a different, though related, sense; there are only a small number of people in it, or in its upper echelons, as Lodge portrays them here. Aside from coincidence, it is a comment on the narrowness of the academic upper reaches that these superstars know each other. The central focus of this smallness is the UNESCO chair in literary criticism, an immensely desirable position which is to be filled on the recommendation of famous literary critic Arthur Kingfisher. It will carry a tax-free salary of $100,000, will not require its occupant to move anywhere, since it is a notional chair, will carry no duties and, of course, will make the person who wins it the most prestigious professor of Literature in the world. The pursuit of this grail occupies most of the upper-level academics in the novel, including Morris Zapp; Fulvia Morgana, an Italian Marxist critic; Michel Tardieu, a French narratologist; Siegfried von Turpitz, a sinister German reception-theorist; and Rudyard Parkinson, a Cambridge fogey. In a typical turn, Philip Swallow's name appears on the short-list, though this is a maneuver against Morris Zapp.

And, though the contestants expend enormous energy and anxiety on this pursuit, it is hardly of earth-shaking importance. Even in 1979 $100,000 was no king's ransom, judged by standards other than those of the academic world. It has been said that the reason academic disputes

84

are so bitter is that the stakes are so small. In Lodge's words, "to the worldly eye the issues which preoccupy academics often seem comically disproportionate to the passions they arouse" (WO 171). And the UNESCO chair is, arguably, a small prize for the ordeals – the conniving, the cringing, the bootlicking and backstabbing – which people will undergo in order to gain it. Thus this world is small in another way.

As these remarks suggest, this novel has a dual focus. One of its major subjects is the small world of high-level academic travel, conferencing, and power-mongering, and the related worlds (also small) of book-publishing and book-reviewing. The other focus is on an individual quest, the quester in this case being Persse McGarrigle. The first body of material, the broad, comic, satiric view of the small world, is driven primarily by the drive for power, only secondarily on the drive for sex (the two determinants of action in the academy, according to Lodge [WO 170]). This part of the book uses ironic juxtapositions and rich coincidences to expose the human frailties of the academics. It is romantic in its freedom from the laws of probability which would otherwise rule out the extensive play of coincidences; it is romantic in being plot-rich, character-diffuse, multifarious and multi-foliate; and it is romantic, finally, in exploiting very cleverly the parallel which Lodge has noted between modern academic travellers and medieval pilgrims. He explains that

> The modern conference resembles the pilgrimage of medieval
> Christendom in that it allows the participants to indulge themselves
> in all the pleasures and diversions of travel while appearing to be
> austerely bent on self-improvement. (1)

But really it is more than this. The conferees are all pilgrims, or put another way, questers. Their quests or pilgrimages are, as the foregoing analogy suggests, very much products of mixed motives, but all are in quest of something. For the elevated, the mighty paladins like Morris Zapp and Fulvia Morgana, the quest is for fame and the ego-satisfaction of international reknown; for smaller fry, the squires like Rodney Wainwright and Philip Swallow, the quest is for occasional escape from tedium, for a momentary glimpse of the empyrean.

And it is this constant motif of questing or searching by which the broad satire of academia is organized. This novel far more than *Changing Places* approaches the scope of a comic *anatomy* of the academic world. It is filled with characters from the academic and literary worlds, almost all of whom are quirky. They figure in odd little vignettes; Felix Skinner, publisher of several of the writers in *Small World*, including Philip Swallow's *Hazlitt and the Common Reader*, discovers during a strenuous afternoon sex bout with his secretary in the storeroom that Philip Swallow's book has never been reviewed because the review copies were never sent out. The same thing happened to David Lodge's *The British Museum is Falling Down*, though the discovery was less sensational. Here, Felix Skinner's attempts to repair the situation, including his smooth evasions as he solicits reviews for an out-of-date book, his engineering of favorable notices, and even Rudyard Parkinson's decision to use a review of Swallow's book in the *Times Literary Supplement* as a weapon against Morris Zapp's claims to the UNESCO chair, thus accidentally elevating Swallow instead of himself into the candidacy: all these are part of a slyly funny view of the literary world at work.

Similarly Lodge has nicely picked up the careers of several of the characters of *Changing Places*, locating them further along the trajectory established there. Howard Ringbaum is an unpleasantly competitive man who destroyed his chances for tenure at Euphoric State when he claimed, while playing a game of Humiliation started by Philip Swallow, that he had never read *Hamlet*. Now, emerging from the wilderness (Southern Illinois University) to attend Morris Zapp's conference in Tel Aviv, he is grimly competitive still, but now in the sexual sphere. He is determined to belong to the "Mile High Club, an exclusive confraternity of men who have achieved sexual congress while airborne" [90] and pesters his wife Thelma to help him qualify. Later in Israel he demands sex in a cable car at Masada.

Another familiar character is Robin Dempsey of the English department of Rummidge. In *Changing Places* he is disappointed when the appointment as senior lecturer, for which he is most eligible on grounds of scholarly work, goes to Philip Swallow instead, primarily because of Zapp's recommendation. Now we find that he has left Rummidge and moved to a new university in Darlington, where he has taken up computer-assisted analysis of style. He has coded all of Ronald Frobisher's work, for instance, and discovered among other traits that Frobisher's favorite word is "grease." Had he read Lodge's *Language of Fiction* Dempsey would have learned that

> the most frequently recurring word in a given text is not necessarily the most significant word. If it were, computers could perform the initial critical task for us. (LF 85).

The point about Robin Dempsey is exactly his failure of critical intel-
ligence and his inability to distinguish between computers and human
beings, and thus we are not surprised to see him spending all his time
confessing his problems and needs to an interactive computer program
which eventually (rigged by the technician) tells him to kill himself.

Other characters illustrate the more common human frailties of
academics, and of course of everybody else: hypocrisy, self-absorption,
laziness, careerism, insincerity, sexual infidelity, ingratitude. Unlike some
readers of this novel, I do not see Lodge as assigning these faults exclusively
to academia, or suggesting that they are more rampant there than in other
areas of human life. He does not hate any of his characters; he is amused
by them, tolerant of their human weaknesses, but they do have the full
range of human weaknesses.

* * * * *

There is one character who is *not* part of the overall pattern I have been
describing as the satire on academic life. He is the protagonist of the most
crucially romantic plot line, the part which most exploits what Hawthorne
calls the "material," that is, the traditional and mythic plot-stuff of
Romance, to which the Romancer lays claim. There is one person in this
small world whose motives are uncomplicated, who pursues one thing and
it for pure reasons, who is not greedy, ambitious, or mean. That is the only
"hero" available here, Persse McGarrigle.

The name tells us that Persse is Perceval, though I think it also suggests
Perseus. Perhaps Persse thinks he is Perseus but is actually Perceval. He
wants to rescue Andromeda; but instead he is fated to be the innocent
knight who asks the question which heals the Grail king of his sexual wound
and restores health to the world over which he presides.

This is a strikingly good conceit for the novel. Lodge explains that for
some time after he began planning a novel about the world of international
scholarship, he lacked a structural principle to provide unity; finally he
thought of the Grail legend, and particularly "of T. S. Eliot's use of the
Grail legend in *The Waste Land* as structural device comparable to Joyce's
use of the *Odyssey* – the Grail legend as reinterpreted by Jessie Weston in
her book *From Ritual to Romance*" (WO 73). In developing the idea, Lodge
clearly has a good bit of fun. For instance, Persse often encounters an
elderly scholar named Miss Sybil Maiden, a former student of Jessie
Weston's, who helpfully glosses his interests and his behavior in terms of
ritual and romance. Likewise, at the still center of the turning world of

high-powered literary scholarship, sits Arthur Kingfisher, the most eminent critic in the world, but now maimed and impotent; equally unable to have an erection or an original idea.

At the conference with which the book opens Persse meets Angelica Pabst, immediately falls in love with her, and sets out on the quest which will lead him around the world and finally to the waste land (the annual convention of the Modern Language Association). Like Perceval, Persse is innocent almost to the point of ignorance; from an agricultural college in Ireland, he has never heard of structuralism, and he is, moreover, a virgin who believes in premarital chastity for both sexes.

Persse's pursuit of Angelica nicely counterpoints the multiple strands of plot having to do with the ambitions and foibles of the literary world. He keeps encountering these other scholars (some of whom, true to Romance convention, prove to be aiding figures—Morris Zapp, Sybil Maiden—while others are opposing figures—Robin Dempsey, Siegfried von Turpitz) because Angelica goes to all the conferences. Her academic background, like so much else about her, is mysterious, but she almost miraculously appears wherever scholarship is afoot, listening to papers particularly if they are about Romance, then disappearing just out of Persse's eager grasp. Along the way Lodge canvasses other works for Romance motifs and allusions, including, most importantly, *The Waste Land*, "The Eve of St. Agnes," and *The Faerie Queene*. There are identical twins, one "good" and one "bad," with distinguishing birthmarks. There are confusions and mistaken identities (two McGarrigles, for instance) and surprises about parentage. There are, of course, plenty of coincidences. There is even a ticket agent at Heathrow who spells Miss Maiden as *ficelle*, reading up on Romance and giving exposition to Persse as he passes through on his Quest. And there is the triumphant moment at the Modern Language Association meeting when Persse asks the miraculous healing question to the assembled knights of academia, the question which restores both sexual and intellectual potency to Arthur Kingfisher, turns Manhattan December into spring, and heals the wounds (writer's block) of Desiree Zapp and Ronald Frobisher. He does not win Angelica; she has never been the real object of his quest, much as he thought she was, and as the book ends he is off on another pursuit.

Along the way there is, as we would expect, some metafictional play from the author, some reminders of the fictiveness of the book we are reading. The conventions of romance, its exuberant defiance of the expectations of grim realism, its coincidences, its "unrealistic" naming (Arthur Kingfisher, Sybil Maiden), its dedication to beauty and variety instead of verisimilitude and probability, all remind us continually of the fictionality of *Small World*.

There are fewer, however, of David Lodge's metafictional reminders, of the sort we have come to expect from *Changing Places* and *How Far Can You Go?* In *Working with Structuralism* he lists characteristic post-modernist devices for shocking the reader like

> combining in one work the apparently factual and the obviously fictional, introducing the author and the question of authorship into the text, and exposing conventions in the act of using them. (15)

It is easy to see how common such practices are in *How Far Can You Go?* But *Small World* is less interested in such effects. Thus, though apparently factual matters like the Modern Language Association convention and the *Times Literary Supplement* are brought into the book, this is a completely traditional means to solidity of specification. Real literary critics and theorists are *mentioned*, but all the ones who actually appear are safely fictional. There is a real world lurking behind the fictional one here, in the sense that Rummidge is a rough representation of Birmingham, and many readers read *Small World* as a *roman à clef* and propose to identify who Fulvia Morgana, for instance, really is. But again, this is fairly conventional. Now, if Lodge had had Fulvia Morgana a member of the same panel as Jacques Derrida, this would have mixed more piquantly the real and the fictional. As for exposing conventions in the act of using them, it seems to me that Lodge is more interested in the use he can make of romance conventions than in the possibility of exposing them. Exposing them for what, anyway? Unrealistic? Old-fashioned? Would such an exposure be worth the trouble it would take to conduct it? No, the employment of romance conventions is no satire on them. It is, of course, a knowing one, and there are, from time to time, scholarly statements about romance which, so far as they are commentary on the novel in which they actually appear, do provide some of the self-reference of the postmodernist novel. For instance, Cheryl Summerbee, the Heathrow ticket agent who has been studying romance, presumably in support of her unsuspected love for Persse McGarrigle, explains

> Real romance is a pre-novelistic kind of narrative. It's full of adventure and coincidence and surprises and marvels, and has lots of characters who are lost or enchanted or wandering about looking for each other, or for the Grail, or something like that. Of course,

they're often in love too . . . . (258)

And Angelica, the mysterious object of Persse's search, delivers a paper at the Modern Language Association in which, while developing an analogy between romance and female orgasm which profoundly shocks Persse, makes the following remarks which apply very accurately to *Small World*:

> It has not one climax but many, the pleasure of this text comes and comes and comes again. No sooner is one crisis in the fortunes of the hero averted than a new one presents itself; no sooner has one mystery been solved than another is raised; no sooner has one adventure been concluded than another begins. (322-23)

Lodge's other postmodernist device, introducing the author and the question of authorship into the text, is one which, as we have seen, is used boldly and tellingly in *How Far Can You Go?* It figures very little here. There are a couple of inside jokes — as for instance, when Philip Swallow's book suffers the same fate as one of Lodge's; another, which also requires knowledge outside the novel, occurs in this scene from the MLA cocktail party near the end of the novel. Almost everybody in the novel has turned up in New York, and the cocktail party brings them together. Persse encounters

> a shortish dark-haired man standing nearby with a bottle of champagne in his hand, talking to a tallish dark-haired man smoking a pipe. "If I can have Eastern Europe," the tallish man was saying in an English accent, "you can have the rest of the world." "All right," said the shortish man, "but I daresay people will still get us mixed up."
> "Are they publishers too?" Persse whispered.
> "No, novelists," said Felix Skinner. (331-32)

The two men are David Lodge and Malcolm Bradbury. To recognize this one has to know what they look like, to know that Bradbury's *Rates of Exchange* is in some ways similar to *Small World* but is set in an unnamed Eastern European country, while *Small World* is, as we realize, set everywhere else, and to be aware of the frequent mixing up of these two novelists, old friends and colleagues and both authors of several campus novels. This little vignette is both self-deprecating and, I believe, a slightly acid comment on Lodge and Bradbury's critics. But it is slight.

There is no requirement, certainly, that David Lodge write books which contain postmodernist elements. His unwillingness to keep following the formula is honorable and admirable. *Small World* has riches enough in it. And yet I find it a slightly disappointing book compared to the two which preceded it. It is not as funny as *Changing Places*, and it is not as exciting in technique as *How Far Can You Go?* It has a less vigorous satiric touch than the former of these books, and less profundity on serious issues than the latter. The form is not as interesting, not as architecturally exciting as what Lodge has achieved in other ensemble novels. The broad canvas along with the explicit dedication to romance means an attenuation of character, always a risk with this author. Philip Swallow and Morris Zapp lose dimensionality here, without a compensating development of any other character, even Persse McGarrigle. And the knowledge of how people behave at the highest levels of the academic world, the "inside information" which David Lodge certainly has and for which many people seem to have read the book, remains fairly broad and unsurprising. That people go to conferences to advance their careers and slake their lust as well as to learn about literature, that many papers are dull repetitive things to which nobody listens, and that professors are at least as ambitious as members of other professions, these are not revelations, unless it is to a naive public for which *Small World* is a searing exposé. The story which publicized the ITV dramatization of *Small World* was headlined "Scholars with sex on the brain." This novel will be most striking to those readers for whom that phrase contains an unthinkable, or at least previously unthought, paradox.

My reservations about *Small World* are in part really reservations about its reception, that is, about the readers and reviewers for whom this is the first really important David Lodge book. I do not think it is, or even a particular improvement over those which preceded it. But the public recognition, nomination for literary prizes, and wider sales and readership were nonetheless, even if belated, well deserved.

91

Chapter Ten

THE CONDITION OF ENGLAND
NICE WORK

David Lodge's most recent novel was published in September 1988. Like *Small World*, it was shortlisted for the Booker Prize. And, though it lost out to Peter Carey's *Oscar and Lucinda*, the judges mentioned it by name as one of the two "runners up." These are signs of Lodge's growing reputation, as is the pre-publication decision by the BBC to broadcast a dramatized version of the book written by the author. Another may be found in the growing animus which appears in some of the reviews and public comments about this book. Complaints that he has written another novel about academics, for instance, seem based on the assumption that this is a subject which, unlike business or espionage or war, has a very narrow specialized appeal; moreover, though one of the two main characters in this book is a college don, it is hardly an academic novel in the same way as *Changing Places* or *Small World*.

The announcement that he was finishing a book "featuring Rummidge, Zapp and Swallow once again" was, perhaps, a somewhat worrying development: was this altogether a good idea? Zapp and Swallow had, after all, lost a bit of their vitality between *Changing Places* and *Small World*, and to bring them out again might even be justifiably called exploitation, particularly after the success of *Small World*. Was David Lodge climbing on his own bandwagon?

The result completely vindicates the recycling of Zapp and Swallow. They are among the least important characters in this novel. It is poised between two worlds, the industrial and the academic, and the academic world is again the Department of English at Rummidge University. This university is, as the Author's Note makes clear, a fictional equivalent of the University of Birmingham, which is where Lodge spent his entire academic career. More important for the reader who may know nothing first hand about Birmingham, it is the same Rummidge of *Changing Places* and *Small World*, seventeen and seven years on respectively, and our ability to register changes in academia by the changes in Rummidge is an added benefit of the author's decision to set his book there. Some of the characters are the same; Bob Busby and Rupert Sutcliffe reappear, suitably aged but otherwise going on as we saw them in *Changing Places*. The role of Philip Swallow is both funny and sad. More than any other character he registers the toll of advancing years and bad times. He has aged greatly; the dapper *Small World*-era Swallow, the increasingly smooth operator, he of the neatly trimmed silver beard and the unbelievable wild love affairs, is now "a tall, thin, stooped man, with silvery grey hair, deeply receding at the temples, curling over his collar at the back . . .tired and careworn and slightly seedy" (36, 38). Moreover he has developed an odd sort of deafness in the throes of which he hears vowels just fine but cannot discriminate consonants, so that he is always mistaking "picket" for "wicket," and "cup of tea" for "cup of pee." It is hard to take him seriously any more.

Which does not mean that he isn't in a serious position. For, continuing the irresistible and almost totally undeserved rise which he began by being promoted to Senior Lecturer in *Changing Places*, and mentioned for the UNESCO chair in *Small World*, he is now Dean of the Faculty of Arts. By the time he achieves this rank, however, it has become not worth having — Swallow's rueful way of calling his domain sweet FA, a slang term for something worthless, is his only attempt at humor — because his main role is to preside over the retrenchment and decline of the university.

What I am saying about Philip Swallow is that in this book he is more of a symbol than a character: important primarily as a metonymy or a synecdoche for the aging and decline of the British University system. Morris Zapp, who also makes an appearance, may also be seen as a representative figure, in this case of the U.S. higher education/literary criticism system, of which he is so luminary a part. Unlike Swallow, who can no longer get a grant to travel abroad, Morris is still on the go to conferences, still receiving the highest salary in the Humanities in his university. His representative function is clear in the explanation of how he affects Robyn Penrose, the promising young scholar who seems to have no future in the University despite her promise:

> there was something about Morris Zapp that inspired hope. He had blown into the jaded, demoralized atmosphere of Rummidge University like an invigorating breeze, intimating that there were still places in the world where scholars and critics pursued their professional goals with zestful confidence, where conferences multiplied and grants were to be had to attend them, where conversation at academic parties was more likely to be about the latest controversial book or article than about the latest scaling-down of departmental maintenance grants. (235)

* * * * *

Why this concern with Swallow and Zapp as representatives? Because *Nice Work* is something different from any of Lodge's earlier books. It is a "Condition of England" novel.

The first "condition of England" novels, written in the 1840s, were about industry. So is David Lodge's, at least in part. In what seems a move towards a broader scope for his novels, he takes on the condition of British manufacturing, in this case the steel industry, and its decline. The inclusion of manufacturing serves many purposes. One is, presumably, to avoid the charge of narrow, mandarin elitism which always threatens the academic novel. Another is to provide a good foil for the academic world; the parallels between the factory and the university, questions of productivity, retrenchment, conditions of work, and "rationalization" are cleverly managed (both J. Pringle and Sons Casting and General Engineering and Rummidge University experience one-day strikes, for instance). And clearly a good deal of research has gone into this, for Lodge writes knowledgeably about how foundries work, what castings are, and precisely how dangerous and unpleasant the work is.

This book, then, goes beyond academia; it is about England in 1986. To be sure, the academy, along with the factory, is one of the representative institutions in Lodge's anatomy of England; but they are just that, representative institutions.

It is a self-consciously old-fashioned novel; its author has described it as "a kind of mixture of a novel of ideas and a comedy of manners" (Moseley), and its overt alignment with the condition of England novel, and writers like Dickens, Charlotte Brontë, and Mrs. Gaskell, is another conspicuous reference to the tradition of the novel. As lecturer Robyn Penrose, an expert in the Victorian industrial novel as well as in contemporary literary theory, explains to her class:

> they dealt with social and economic problems arising out of the Industrial Revolution, and in some cases described the nature of factory work. In their own time they were often called "Condition of England Novels," because they addressed themselves directly to the state of the nation. They are novels in which the main characters debate topical social and economic issues as well as fall in and out of love, marry and have children, pursue careers, make or lose their fortunes, and do all the other things that characters do in more conventional novels. (45)

This description fails only in suggesting, in its last phrase, that there

94

was something "unconventional" about this class of novels. Though the subject matter was unusual for its time, a fact of which the authors were quite conscious and to which they sometimes pointed in their titles or subtitles (*Mary Barton: A Tale of Manchester Life*), still the plotting and other novelistic features were conventional. Lodge pays tribute to this conventionality in *Nice Work*; though the subject, the twinning of academia and industry, is a novelty, still the construction of the novel is conventional in an almost nineteenth century way. There are paired and contrapuntal narratives and a happy ending which not only ties up loose ends and roughly satisfies the demands of poetic justice, but even makes creaky (and, I suppose, joky) use of the unknown uncle in Australia who dies providentially leaving the heroine the money which solves her immediate problems.

Nice Work, like others of David Lodge's novels, acknowledges its debts openly. In addition to the enclosed commentary on the genre to which it belongs, contained in Robyn Penrose's lecture on the Condition of England novels, it has epigraphs from Mrs. Gaskell's *North and South*, Dickens's *Hard Times*, Charlotte Brontë's *Shirley*, and Disraeli's *Sybil, or The Two Nations*. Furthermore the details of the novel themselves constitute allusion to several of these novels; the two realms at the heart of *Nice Work*, for instance — the industrial and the academic — are as sharply divided, as truly two nations, as the rich and poor in Disraeli's time. One of Lodge's epigraphs quotes from *Sybil*; Disraeli's character Morley explains that Queen Victoria rules over

> Two nations; between whom there is no intercourse and no sympathy; who are as ignorant of each other's habits, thoughts, and feelings, as if they were dwellers in different zones, or inhabitants of different planets; who are formed by a different breeding, and fed by different food, and ordered by different manners . . .

The same divisions separate the world of the factory from the world of the university in *Nice Work*. The author has touched in very nicely the differences between Robyn Penrose and Vic Wilcox, the representatives of the two nations here, in the food they eat, the newspapers they read, their tastes in music, home decoration, leisure pursuits, and even alarm clocks. Perhaps in tribute to Mrs. Gaskell's novel, he has also established them as representative of North and South. Vic is a lifelong inhabitant of the industrial midlands, having grown up in a terraced house in Rummidge, where his old father still lives. Robyn is a child of southern England — actually of Australia, from which her family moved her when she was five to the South Coast of England. Her father is himself a don; she is cosmopolitan, has no particular attachment to her parents' home, and is a sort of emblematic figure of the upper-middle-class southerner, prosperous by way of intellectual work rather than producing goods, unreflecting about money and where it comes from because an easy life, and nice work, have kept her indifferent to such Rummidgy preoccupations.

I have remarked before on the resonance of David Lodge's titles — *Changing Places*, for instance — and *Nice Work*, though not of that complex plurisignification, is another rich title, despite its being a second choice. Originally the book was to be called *Shadow Work*, in reference to the scheme by which Robyn Penrose and Vic Wilcox shadow each other at work and learn about life on the other side of the divide. The publishers insisted on the change to *Nice Work*, which actually means much more. At one point Vic Wilcox uses the cliché. In a very funny bit, he accompanies Robyn to the Senior Common Room and sees, to his amazement, the academic staff knocking off at midmorning to drink coffee, "doss around," and discuss gardening problems.

> Robyn looked at her colleagues lounging in easy chairs, smiling and chatting to each other, or browsing through the newspapers and weekly reviews, as they drank their coffee and nibbled their biscuits. She suddenly saw this familiar spectacle through an outsider's eyes, and almost blushed. "We all have our own work to do," she said. "It's up to us how we do it."
> "If you don't start till ten and you knock off for a coffee-break at eleven," said Vic, "I don't see where you find the time." (247)

Vic next accompanies Robyn to a committee meeting, where he listens to Philip Swallow's explanation of tenure and the difficulty of rationalizing universities when nobody can be made redundant without his consent. "'Well,' said Vic, 'It's nice work if you can get it'" (249).

This comment on academic life — this suggestion that, as work, it is a bit of a fraud — is one which troubles Robyn a bit. Because, after all, academic work *is* nice work. And what observation of the foundry dramatically points out is that for most of the work force, the phrase "nice work" is an oxymoron. Work is not meant to be nice; it's work. Robyn comes to realize how fortunate she is to make her living by something which she also enjoys, as she recognizes the almost hellish conditions under which Vic Wilcox's employees earn their bread.

From time to time she gives way to a Utopian fantasy that actualizes her earlier angry retort "Model industry on universities. Make factories collegiate institutions" (246). Her mind wanders during the committee meeting, first to the horrible engineering works in West Wallsbury, where the men are doing work that is anything but nice in conditions which contrast sharply with her senior common room.

> Instead of letting them go back into that hell-hole, she transported them, in her imagination, to the campus: the entire workforce — labourers, craftsmen, supervisors, managers, directors, secretaries and cleaners and cooks, in their grease-stiff dungarees and soiled overalls and chain-store frocks and striped suits — brought them in buses across the city, and unloaded them at the gates of the campus, and let them wander through it in a long procession, like a lost army, headed by Danny Ram and the two Sikhs from the cupola and the giant black from the knockout, their eyes rolling white in their swarthy, soot-blackened faces, as they stared about them with bewildered curiosity at the fine buildings and the trees and the flowerbeds and lawns, and at the beautiful young people at work or play all around them. And the beautiful young people and their teachers stopped dallying and disputing and got to their feet and came forward to greet the people from the factory, shook their hands and made them welcome, and a hundred small seminar groups formed on the grass, composed half of students and lecturers and half of workers and managers, to exchange ideas on how the values of the university and the imperatives of commerce might be reconciled and more equitably managed to the benefit of the whole of society. (249-50)

Only connect. It is the aim of the shadow scheme, and it has its limited success there. But Robyn's vision suffers still from her own limitations, her insistence that workers and students must connect by turning the workers into students. And at the end of the day, Robyn recognizes that workers and students, university and factory, the the two nations are not going to be joined by any such sentimental and facile reconciliation.

This description of the novel should demonstrate that it is one of David Lodge's binary fictions. That is, it counterposes two worlds and two metonymic characters from those worlds, in a searching, occasionally ironic counterpoint. It is linked, then, to *Ginger, You're Barmy* and *Changing Places*. And Lodge has always been interested in the contrast and opposition, but also in the similarity and interplay of apparently contrasting positions and personalities. Moreover, there is always some change, some movement toward an exchange of roles and commitments. Jon Browne in *Ginger* takes on not only Mike Brady's girl but his seriousness; in *The Picturegoers* Mark Underwood and Clare Mallory cross each other as he moves towards Catholicism, she towards secularism. Philip Swallow becomes more American, Morris Zapp more English. And so on.

Here the premise is that a hard-headed man of industry and a somewhat rarified university lecturer (also hard-headed, but in an entirely different way) are paired with each other, and the novel consists of the results and ramifications of that pairing. Much of the interest derives from cross-cultural shocks and contrasts. Robyn Penrose has hardly even seen a factory and knows nothing about the lives of the proletarians for whom, as a sort of trendy socialist, she "cares." Vic Wilcox has nothing but contempt for the lives of university staff and students, who in his view perform no vital service, create no wealth, but enjoy a soft life at the expense of those who do. (Perceptions of university life in this novel, as in the real world, are colored by television shows like *Small World* and *Porterhouse Blue*; Vic Wilcox's dad's comment on "university dongs" is "I seen films on the telly. All sorts of queer folk, carrying on with each other something chronic").(172) The clash of preconceptions and misconceptions produces some comedy but, more important, a softening and complicating of positions, an advance in sympathy, a rejection of stereotypes, a humanization of both partners in the shadow scheme.

Thus Robyn Penrose not only becomes interested in and sympathetic to the laborers in Pringle's, but even begins to see the human faces of the capitalist bosses and entrepreneurs. Perhaps her most vital lesson from her association with Vic is the inescapability of money. She is in the habit (like other academics, perhaps) of offering breezily simple answers to complex questions of social policy. In the face of her pleasure over a one-day staff strike against higher education cuts, he points out, unanswerably, that such a strike hurts no one and actually costs money, thus exacerbating the financial crisis which produced the cuts against which the staff were striking. Moreover, when Robyn argues that more university positions should be made available, rather than fewer, Vic again points out the costs — higher taxes and a loss of jobs in manufacturing. Robyn later turns the argument against her lover, Charles, another deconstructionist, when she asks "Why should society pay to be told people don't mean what they say or say what they mean?" (153)

Vic Wilcox moves even more than Robyn Penrose, though this is partly because he falls in love with her. He almost never reads, when the book begins, and is not only uneducated in the usual sense, but truculent about it. By the end he is knowledgeable about the difference between metaphor and metonymy (an interest shared by Robyn Penrose and David Lodge) and reads the novels of the Brontës, Tennyson's poetry, and *Daniel Deronda*. Her attempt to deconstruct love fails with him, though, and to a certain extent no longer even convinces her.

The convergence of the twain should not be exaggerated or sentimentalized, and Lodge stops well short of that, at a point where Robyn Penrose is still a lecturer, Vic Wilcox still a businessman in the engineering industry. The end of the novel explicitly rejects any idea that the two nations can come together, yet, on equal terms. As Robyn thinks, quoting Stephen Blackpool in *Hard Times*, it is "aw a muddle," and muddle it remains even after Robyn and Vic's shadowing is over.

It must be tempting, in constructing a dialectical plot such as this one, to weight one or the other side of the equation, to let one side "win." It is part of Lodge's honorable liberal balance, his acceptance of muddle, his ability to see both sides of questions and his willingness to do justice to them, that this contrast is so even. Robyn Penrose in some measure triumphs, as her needs are fulfilled while Vic Wilcox must suffer some disruption; but in the argument between academia and industry, and the related argument between literary theory and realism, Vic seems to me to have the stronger hand. Robyn Penrose is close to David Lodge in a number of ways more important than her employment at Rummidge University, and when she speaks of metaphor and metonymy she could be quoting from *The Modes of Modern Writing*; but the counterclaims of that very different world of Vic Wilcox's inhabiting are presented at least as compellingly. Like another Victorian novelist, George Eliot, David Lodge seems less intent on showing "the" truth and exploding error than on enlarging the bounds of human sympathy.

Just as Lodge in his critical work likes to think in binary terms (metaphor and metonymy, modern and contemporary, symbolist and realist) but refuses to endorse one choice at the expense of the other: so in his fictions. I think the metaphor/metonymy dualism underlies his characterization; Robyn Penrose is a metaphorical character, Vic Wilcox a metonymic one. Both are "right."

David Lodge's greatest strength as a novelist, I have previously insisted, is his mastery of structure and pattern. This is another novel, clearly, which makes use of that skill. His corresponding weakness is in the creation of strong and convincing characters. This weakness is also important in *Nice*

Work, partly because of Lodge's ambitious turn to a different sort of novel. This book calls for two strong characters in Vic and Robyn, because of their absolute centrality; and its determination to be a sort of classic realistic novel of social life and moral responsibility – like *Shirley* and *Hard Times* and *North and South*, with which it aligns itself – also requires a quality of characterization which, unfortunately, it does not achieve. It is of less importance that the secondary characters, Robyn's Charles or her feminist friend Penny Black, or Vic Wilcox's wife, secretary, daughter and sons, are more or less stereotypes. They are after all the minor characters, part of the comic counterpart of the serious interplay at the heart of the book. It is regrettable, though, that Vic and Robyn fail to live more fully than they do. They are not stereotypes, but they are not vital enough.

In a comic novel, or an ensemble novel, this would matter less. Philip Swallow and Morris Zapp are somewhat two-dimensional men, flat characters with more than a few stereotypical traits, but they inhabit a different kind of novel. The people in *How Far Can You Go?* won't bear comparison with Charlotte Brontë's or Elizabeth Gaskells' creations, either, but their multiplicity makes this less damaging. *Nice Work*, despite its comic elements, is a primarily serious book, based strongly on its two main characters, and their shortage of vitality is necessarily a defect.

But not a crippling one. We must admire the ambition of the aim, the (largely successful) creation of a plot and a milieu which symbolize the condition of England, the art and wit and architechtonics, and the author's broad humane sympathy. Whether this marks out a new direction entirely for David Lodge, or whether (as in the past) he will alternate works of more serious realism with comedy, this novel again proves his determination to expand and shows him, with his eighth book, as powerful as ever.

Chapter Eleven

LODGE'S CRITICISM

In addition to writing novels David Lodge has had a busy career as a literary scholar and critic. He is the author of short books on two major twentieth-century English Catholic novelists — Graham Greene and Evelyn Waugh — published in the Columbia Essays on Modern Writers Series by Columbia University Press. He has edited and written introductions to several classic novels. His *Twentieth Century Literary Criticism: A Reader*, which appeared in 1972, is a collection of major texts; it has recently been complemented by *Modern Criticism and Theory: a Reader*, which Lodge describes as "a kind of swan-song of my academic career" (Moseley). But his major work is in his four books of literary criticism and theory and his one volume of occasional essays, many of them criticism or at least book reviews. These are, respectively, *Language of Fiction: Essays in Criticism and Verbal Analysis of the English Novel* (1966); *The Novelist at the Crossroads and Other Essays on Fiction and Criticism* (1971); *The Modes of Modern Writing: Metaphor, Metonymy, and the Typology of Modern Literature* (1977); *Working with Structuralism: Essays and Reviews on Nineteenth and Twentieth-Century Literature* (1981); and *Write On: Occasional Essays '65-'85* (1986).

The last-named is a book unlike anything else he has written; it is much more informal — particularly in the first half, entitled "Personal and Descriptive" — and the essays in the second half, called "Literary and Critical," are *very* occasional, being almost entirely reprinted reviews. Several of these connect nicely with his other critical work; for instance, reviews of Norman Mailer and Truman Capote continue his interest in the "non-fiction" novel, treated at length in *The Novelist at the Crossroads*; there is some discussion of structuralism, about which he writes more "academically" elsewhere; and one of the reviews is illuminating on the campus novel, which is of course one of David Lodge's own specialties.

But the real interest in this book comes from its relaxed, conversational tone and its forthright discussions of the author's life and how the life relates to the novels. Of particular interest are "The Bowling Alley and the Sun *or* How I Learned to Stop Worrying and Love America," "My Joyce," "Memories of a Catholic Childhood," "Why Do I Write?" and a review called "The Limits of the Movement." All these shed much light on the origins of the novelist and the genesis of the novels, and I have learned much from them.

The four more rigorously academic books which preceded *Write On* divide into two groups. The first and third, *Language of Fiction* and *The Modes of Modern Writing*, are more sustained and theoretical studies; *The Novelist at the Crossroads* and *Working with Structuralism* are somewhat occasional themselves, collections of diverse essays, addresses, and reviews linked very loosely to the topics announced in the titles.

A glance at the biographical facts will suggest why *Language of Fiction* is the most unified of these books; it is the only one whose author was a relatively unknown lecturer at Birmingham University, a novelist without a large reputation and a critic with almost none. *Language of Fiction* quickly changed that; it was recognized as an important contribution to criticism of prose fiction. It was as the author of *Language of Fiction* that David Lodge became one of the better known Anglo-American critics; that he was invited to contribute to things like the series "Towards a Poetics of Fiction" in the first volume of *Novel: A Forum on Fiction*; that, ultimately, he found himself at the 1978 Modern Language Association, the 1979 James Joyce Symposium, and other similar conclaves which punctuate *Small World*.

Language of Fiction has two parts. The first is theoretical and polemical. Here the author is determined to establish that criticism of the novel should be criticism of its language. He begins with a survey of opinions on the language of fiction, starting with I. A. Richards and touching on most well-known modern discussions of the novelist's medium. He continues with a discussion of stylistics; and then provides his own critical credo, including both principles and methods. Here he emphasizes the analysis of repetition (of keywords, for instance) in linguistic criticism of the novel.

Part Two of the book is practical criticism; here, in seven chapters mostly on nineteenth-century classic novels, he shows how linguistic criticism works. From the evidence available, none of these essays had been previously published; they were written for this book, and this explains their appropriateness to the theoretical preparation for them.

The other major theoretical book appeared in 1977. *The Modes of Modern Writing: Metaphor, Metonymy, and the Typology of Modern Literature* is Lodge's most ambitious attempt to create a theory which explains, and contains, the different schools of modern fiction. He has always been interested in typology, and this always, or almost always, takes a dual form. In *Language of Fiction* the essay on the modern and the contemporary begins to deal with the distinction between two ideas of what literature is; as he expresses the same distinction in the first chapter of *The Modes of Modern Writing*, they are one idea that it is language used for purposes of imitation, that is to say, for the making of fictions, and the other stating that it is language used in a way that is aesthetically pleasing, that calls attention to itself as medium. (MMW 1)

This dichotomy is fundamentally the same as the modern/contemporary one as well as the distinction between modernist and antimodernist he makes elsewhere. There are two important points to make about this split.

First, as we would expect from Lodge's essentially liberal, pluralistic approach to literature, he distinguishes between two radically different kinds of literature, but without taking the usual next step: declaring one kind better than the other. Or, as he puts it in a chapter on the *nouvelle critique*:

I have no quarrel with the *nouvelle critique*'s insistence on the primacy of language in the creation and criticism of prose fiction. . . . But I am less impressed by the polemic against realism that absorbs so much of its energy, since this seems to lead us into the same limiting dichotomy between two kinds of fiction, only one of which we are permitted to admire, that we have already traced in Anglo-American criticism. (MMW 65)

It is this openness, this refusal to rule out, on theoretical grounds, the possibility of value in *any* kind of literature, which makes Lodge a humane critic, and which makes him a sensitive interpreter of criticism and fiction which is not only different from his own but in some ways an attack on it.

Now the theoretical basis for *The Modes of Modern Writing* is a distinction found in the writings of Roman Jakobson, and particularly his suggestion that the two poles of literary discourse are connected with the two very different figures of metaphor and metonymy. For David Lodge, metaphor is the figure most associated with modernism; metonymy with antimodernism; metaphor with symbolism, metonymy with realism. This perception leads to a number of interesting analyses, in which, say, Henry James and Arnold Bennett figure as the representatives of metaphor and metonymy, or Dylan Thomas and Philip Larkin.

Lodge uses another concept which comes from the literary criticism of the Prague formalist school (to which Roman Jakobson belonged): *foregrounding*. For Lodge, one of the modes of modern writing is, at any given time, foregrounded, while the other is background. This provides him with a scheme to explain the alternations and fluctuations in modern British writing; he claims, for instance, that in the twenties writing leaned predominantly toward the metaphorical mode; in the thirties, toward the metonymic, and so on. The fifties, the decade of his own development as a writer, was a metonymic period. In this comment on Philip Larkin he sums up the two poles neatly: one mode of modern writing is modernist, symbolist, writerly and metaphoric; the other is antimodernist, realistic, readerly, and metonymic.

The Modes of Modern Writing, like all Lodge's critical work, is amply provided with examples and test cases, and his close readings of representative writers are valuable and interesting, even for readers who may suspect that the metaphor/metonymy scheme is too grand and too absolute to account for the messy experience of reading and writing.

Lodge's other two books of criticism follow a common pattern: one or more powerful and fairly theoretical lead essays, followed by other, more limited, reprinted pieces. *The Novelist at the Crossroads* takes its title from its lead essay, which posits a crisis of a sort in fiction; realism being problematical, the novelist faces a choice between the non-fiction novel and the playfully fictive fabulation; between the paths of Truman Capote and Donald Barthelme. This choice becomes less stark as Lodge introduces another possibility, what he calls the "problem novel" and other critics would call the "self-conscious novel," and he finally concludes that realism is not facing a dead end after all. One unsympathetic reviewer characterizes Lodge's essay thus:

> As a conscientious liberal critic he recommends the novelist at the crossroads to glance hesitantly to the right and to the left and then to keep straight on, in the faith that on or about December 1960 human character did not change. (Parrinder 879)

Though this is funny, and it captures what is conservative in Lodge's position, it is mistaken; though he would regret the loss of realism as a possibility for writers, and does not in fact believe that the realistic novel is now impossible, he likes what he sees, whether he looks to the right or the left. He admires much of the fiction of the fabulators and the non-fiction novelists as well. Here as elsewhere we see the inclusiveness of his tastes. Though he aims at typology, though he likes to classify fictions into (usually two) types, he doesn't dismiss one of them.

The remainder of *The Novelist at the Crossroads* is a miscellany of articles on Catholic novelists (including a reprinting of his 1966 pamphlet on Graham Greene), on Hemingway, Beckett, H. G. Wells, and so on.

Working With Structuralism is the title of Lodge's 1981 book, and a somewhat misleading one. One reviewer charged that it should have been called "Working Around Structuralism." The first section does contain another effort at typology, the essay "Modernism, Antimodernism and Postmodernism," which recapitulates briefly the arguments contained in *The Modes of Modern Writing* and again uses the Jakobsonian metaphor/metonymy dichotomy to separate modernism and antimodernism. He drops this polar opposition to explain postmodernism, which he does largely by an account of its methods — e.g., permutation, randomness, etc. At the end of this essay (originally an inaugural lecture delivered at the University of Birmingham) he asks himself to which camp his own novels belong, and concludes that they are more anti-modernist than anything else but really belong to all three types. The remainder of this book shows why the subtitle is more accurate than the title: *Essays and Reviews on Nineteenth and Twentieth-Century Literature*. This is Lodge's least unified, least impressive volume. Though everything in it shows the good sense, lucidity, and humane qualities of all his nonfiction writing, its overall impact is fairly slight.

And it shows, what is fairly obvious in *The Modes of Modern Writing* as well, that Lodge is interested in structuralism but only up to a point. His own assessment is that he is "a sort of popularizer or domesticator or, some would say, vulgarizer of structuralism, I guess. I'm by no means in the vanguard of it . . ." (Marecki 301). He makes good use of the metaphor/metonymy distinction and of the idea that all literary choices derive meaning only from the system of oppositions of which they are a part, he has little use for Roland Barthes, he is (rightly, in my opinion) suspicious of the obfuscation and elegant mystification of much French structuralist writing, and he draws the line at deconstructionism. He explains that he is unable to accept the decentering of the author; I would suspect that deconstructionism's assault on "liberal humanism" is also distressing to Lodge.

It is not easy to sum up Lodge's accomplishment as a critic. Undoubtedly he is a major figure in the criticism of prose fiction in our time, one whose critical reputation is separate from (and was for a long time greater than) his name as a novelist. Today's climate of literary theory is unreceptive to some of his principles — for instance, the defense of realism, the inclusive rather than exclusive attitude toward different types of writing, the belief in determinate and communicable meaning. His reasonableness, lack of dogmatism, and willingness to grant the claims of competing systems of thought or ideas of literature are intellectually akin to the balance we find in his novels. The same mind that appreciates both Robyn Penrose and Vic Wilcox in *Nice Work* likes both Samuel Beckett and Kingsley Amis, both modernism and antimodernism. The liberal pluralism which works against doctrinaire conclusions may seem, to some, an uncomfortable attempt at an impossible compromise. One unnamed "former colleague" says of him:

> David's work is an attempt to hold on to certain traditional assumptions of the English novel. He uses semi-experimental methods to return to realism. There is a defensiveness about the realistic tradition. Beyond that experimentation there is a great desire to recreate a world that is true. He keeps talking about the futility of what he is doing, nevertheless he insists upon the power of the illusion. (Midgeley 10)

This sounds almost like Beckett's "I can't go on, I'll go on." It is less desperate than that, as we see in Lodge's own self-estimate, which relates his fiction to his criticism:

> If it has occurred to the reader to wonder where I would place my own fiction in this scheme, I would answer, in the spirit of "Animal, Vegetable, or Mineral": basically antimodernist, but with elements of modernism and postmodernism. Rummidge is certainly a metonymic place name, but Euphoric State is a metaphor, and the ending of *Changing Places* is a short circuit. (NC 16)

PRIMARY BIBLIOGRAPHY

About Catholic Authors (London: St. Paul Press, 1957)

The Picturegoers (London: MacGibbon & Kee, 1960)

Ginger, You're Barmy (London: MacGibbon & Kee, 1962; Garden City: Doubleday, 1965; Harmondsworth: Penguin, 1982)

The British Museum is Falling Down (London: MacGibbon & Kee, 1965; New York: Holt Rinehart, 1967; republished London: Secker & Warburg, 1981)

Language of Fiction: Essays in Criticism and Verbal Analysis of the English Novel (London: Routledge & Kegan Paul; New York: Columbia University Press, 1966)

Graham Greene, Columbia Essays on Modern Writers Series, no. 17 (New York & London: Columbia University Press, 1966)

Out of the Shelter (London: Macmillan, 1970; rev. ed. London: Secker & Warburg, 1985; Harmondsworth: Penguin Books, 1986).

The Novelist at the Crossroads and Other Essays on Fiction and Criticism (London: Routledge & Kegan Paul, 1971; Ithaca: Cornell University Press, 1971; Ark paperback 1986).

Evelyn Waugh, Columbia Essays on Modern Writers Series, no. 58 (New York & London: Columbia University Press, 1971)

Changing Places: A Tale of Two Campuses (London: Secker & Warburg, 1975; New York: Penguin, 1978)

The Modes of Modern Writing: Metaphor, Metonymy, and the Typology of Modern Literature (Ithaca: Cornell University Press, 1977; London: Arnold, 1977)

How Far Can You Go? (London: Secker & Warburg, 1980); republished as *Souls and Bodies* (New York: Morrow, 1982).

Working with Structuralism: Essays and Reviews on Nineteenth and Twentieth-Century Literature (London & Boston: Routledge & Kegan Paul, 1981; Ark paperback 1986).

Small World: An Academic Romance (London: Secker & Warburg, 1984; New York: Macmillan, 1984; Harmondsworth: Penguin, 1985)

Write On: Occasional Essays '65-'85 (London: Secker & Warburg, 1986)

Nice Work: A Novel (London: Secker & Warburg, 1988; New York: Viking Press, 1989).

As Editor:

Twentieth Century Literary Criticism: A Reader (London: Longman, 1972).

Modern Criticism and Theory: A Reader (London: Longman, 1988).

* * * * *

Page references for quotations in this book are to the following editions, where more than one is available:
The Picturegoers: McGibbon & Kee, 1960
Ginger, You're Barmy: Penguin, 1984
The British Museum Is Falling Down: Secker & Warburg, 1981
Out of the Shelter: Penguin, 1986
Changing Places: Penguin, 1978
How Far Can You Go?: Secker & Warburg, 1980
Small World: Penguin, 1985
Language of Fiction: Columbia UP, 1966
The Novelist at the Crossroads: Routledge & Kegan Paul, 1971
The Modes of Modern Writing: Edward Arnold, 1977

SECONDARY BIBLIOGRAPHY

Alter, Robert. *Partial Magic: The Novel as a Self-Conscious Genre*. Berkeley: University of California Press, 1975.

Barth, John. "The Literature of Exhaustion." *The Novel Today: Contemporary Writers on Modern Fiction*. Ed. Malcolm Bradbury. Manchester: Manchester UP, 1977.

Bergonzi, Bernard. "A Conspicuous Absentee: The Decline and Fall of the Catholic Novel." *Encounter* 55 (August-September 1980): 44-56.

_____. "David Lodge Interviewed." *Month* 229 (February 1970): 108-116.

_____. *The Situation of the Novel*. London: Macmillan, 1970.

Bradbury, Malcolm. "If Your Books Are Funny, Please Tell Me Where." *New York Times Book Review* (July 17, 1988): 1, 24-26.

_____. *Possibilities: Essays on the State of the Novel*. London: Oxford UP, 1973.

Burden, Robert. "The Novel Interrogates Itself: Parody as Self-Consciousness in Contemporary English Fiction." *The Contemporary English Novel*. Ed. Malcolm Bradbury and David Palmer. New York: Holmes & Meier, 1979.

D'Hoen, Theo. "Fowles, Lodge, and the Problematic Novel." *Dutch Quarterly Review of Anglo-American Letters* 9 (1980): 162-75.

Frye, Northrup. *Anatomy of Criticism: Four Essays*. Princeton: Princeton UP, 1957.

Genette, Gérard. *Narrative Discourse: An Essay in Method*. Trans. Jane E. Lewin. Ithaca: Cornell University Press, 1980.

Haffenden, John. *Novelists in Interview*. London: Methuen, 1985.

Hawthorne, Nathaniel. *The House of the Seven Gables*. New York: Dutton, 1973.

Honan, Park. "David Lodge and the Cinematic Novel in England." *Novel: A Forum on Fiction* 5 (Winter 1972): 167-73.

Jackson, Dennis. "David Lodge (28 January 1935-)" *British Novelists Since 1960, Part 2: A-Z* (Dictionary of Literary Biography, Vol 14). Ed. Jay L. Halia. Detroit: Gale Research, 1983.

McDonnell, Thomas P. Review of *Ginger, You're Barmy. Commonweal* 83 (November 26, 1965): 249-50.

Marecki, Joan E. and Jean W. Ross. "Lodge, David (John) 1935-" *Contemporary Authors* (New Revision Series, Vol 19). Ed. Linda Metzger. Detroit: Gale Research, 1987.

Midgley, Simon. "How David Lodge Changed Places." *Times Higher Education Supplement* (Nov 28, 1980): 10.

Morace, Robert A. *The Dialogic Novels of Malcolm Bradbury and David Lodge*. Carbondale: Southern Illinois UP, 1989.

Moseley, Merritt. Interview with David Lodge. September 12, 1988, Birmingham, England.

O'Shea, Michael J. "David Lodge's Catholic Metafiction." paper presented at the Carolinas Symposium on British Studies, September 1, 1986.

Parrinder, Patrick. Review of *The Novelist at the Crossroads. Modern Language Review* 67 (October 1972): 878-79.

Rabaté, Jean-Michel. "La 'Fin du Roman' et les Fins des Romans." *Études Anglaises: Grande-Bretagne, États-Unis* 36 (1983): 197-212.

Steinmann, Martin Jr. "The Old Novel and the New." *From Jane Austen to Joseph Conrad*. Ed. Robert C. Rathburn and Martin Steinmann, Jr. Minneapolis: University of Minnesota Press, 1958.

Streichsbier, Beata. "Irony in David Lodge's *How Far Can You Go?*" *Wiener Beitrage zur englischen Philologie* 78 (1981): 97-110.

Sutherland, J. A. *Fiction and the Fiction Industry*. London: The Athlone Press, 1978.

INDEX

111

metafiction 13, 39, 42, 44, 66, 71, 80, 89
metaphor 45, 55, 99, 101-106
metonymy 55, 99, 101-106
modernism 12, 55, 103, 105-106

National Service 2, 4, 14, 21, 27-34, 74

parody 35, 37, 39-43, 54, 58
postmodernism 38-39, 75-76, 89-91, 105-106

realism 3, 12, 24, 27, 32, 35, 37-39, 41, 55, 65-66, 68, 76, 88-89, 99-100,
    103-106
romance 38, 82-83, 87-91
Rummidge 7, 59-62, 64-65, 81, 84, 86, 89, 92-96, 99, 106

self-consciousness 3, 35, 42-44, 58, 66, 68, 75, 94, 104